He Satisfies My
SOUL

He Satisfies My
SOUL

A Celebration of God's Creative Gifts for Body, Mind, and Spirit

Dr. Paul Brand
foreword by Philip Yancey

DISCOVERY HOUSE
PUBLISHERS®

Discovery House Publishers is affiliated with RBC Ministries,
Grand Rapids, Michigan.

Requests for permission to quote from this book should be directed to:
Permissions Department, Discovery House Publishers, P.O. Box 3566,
Grand Rapids, MI 49501 or contact us by e-mail at
permissionsdept@dhp.org

Library of Congress Cataloging-in-Publication Data
available on request

Printed in the United States of America
Third printing in 2011

CONTENTS

FOREWORD

I first learned of Dr. Brand because of his stature in the world medical community. I knew that he had surgical procedures named after him, had received the prestigious Albert Lasker1 Award, and was designated Commander of the Order of the British Empire by Queen Elizabeth II. I sought him out, however, mainly because my wife had found in the closet of a medical-supply house an intriguing article he had written on the gift of pain. I had read many books on the problem of pain, but never one describing pain as a gift.

My first visit with Dr. Brand, at a leprosy hospital in Carville, Louisiana, lasted a week. We grabbed bits of conversation between his surgeries, clinical lectures, and animal research. At night in his home, a rented wooden-frame bungalow on the grounds of the hospital, I would share an Indian-style meal with him and his wife, Margaret, an ophthalmologist of some renown. Then Paul Brand would prop up his bare feet (a trademark with him), and I would turn on the tape recorder for discussions that ranged from leprology and theology to world hunger and soil conservation.

During that visit Dr. Brand admitted to me, somewhat shyly, that he had once tried writing a book. He had delivered a series of chapel talks to a medical school in Vellore, India, and other faculty members had encouraged him to write them down for publication. He made the effort, but the material came to only ninety pages, not long enough for a real book. And that was twenty years ago—he hadn't worked on the book since.

I persuaded him to dig through closets and bureau drawers until he located the badly smudged third carbon copy of those chapel talks, and that night I sat up long past midnight reading his astonishing meditations on the human body. I had struck gold. I asked Dr. Brand if we could collaborate, and those ninety pages eventually became two full-length books, *Fearfully and Wonderfully Made* and *In His Image*. Years later, we collaborated on a third book, *The Gift of Pain*.

In my role as journalist, I had interviewed many subjects: sports stars, successful business people, Pulitzer Prize winners, Olympic athletes. But something attracted me to Dr. Brand at a deeper level than I had felt with any other interview subject. I found in him a rich mixture of compassion, scientific precision, theological depth, and spiritual humility. "The glory of God," said the early Christian theologian Irenaeus, "is a fully alive human being." That is what I found in Paul Brand.

We made an odd couple, Dr. Brand and I. When we first met in Carville, I was a young punk in my mid-twenties, with bushy Afro hair; Dr. Brand was a distinguished, silver-haired surgeon characterized by proper British reserve. I was attracted to his humility, his authenticity, and his substance. Most speakers and writers I knew were hitting the circuit, packaging and repackaging the same thoughts in different books and giving the same speeches to different crowds. Meanwhile, Dr. Brand, who had more intellectual and spiritual depth than perhaps anyone I had ever met, was letting his one attempt at writing molder in a closet. That is why I took on the mission to "expose" Dr. Brand.

That task led me to India twice, and also to England, where Dr. Brand had studied medicine. If you want to know the truth about a surgeon, interview his scrub nurses and patients years later. I did that, and found in their recollections of Dr. Brand the same impressions of humility and compassion.

It takes a few pennies a day to arrest leprosy's progress with sulfone drugs. But it takes thousands of dollars, and the painstaking care of skilled professionals, to restore to wholeness a patient in whom the disease had spread unchecked. In India, Dr. Brand began with hands, experimenting with tendon and muscle transfers until he found the best combination to restore a full range of movement. The surgical procedures and rehabilitation stretched over months and sometimes years. He applied similar procedures to feet, correcting the deformities caused by years of walking around without a sense of pain to guide the body in distributing weight and pressure.

New feet and hands gave a leprosy patient the capability to earn a living, but who would hire an employee bearing the scars of the dread disease? Thus Dr. Brand and his wife saw the need to correct the cosmetic damage as well. They studied techniques of plastic surgery on noses and eyes, modifying them to address the special problems of leprosy.

All this elaborate medical care went to "nobodies," victims of leprosy who most commonly made their living from begging. Many who arrived at the hospital looked barely human. Their shoulders slumped, they cringed when other people approached, and the light had faded from their eyes. But months of compassionate treatment from the staff at Vellore could restore that light to their eyes. For years, people had shrunk away from them in terror; at Vellore, nurses and doctors would hold their hands and talk with them. They became human again.

One man I met, Sadan, looked like a miniature version of Gandhi: skinny, balding, perched cross-legged on the edge of a bed. In a high-pitched, singsong voice he told me wrenching stories of past rejection: the classmates who made fun of him in school; the driver who kicked him—literally, with his shoe—off a public bus; the many employers who refused to hire him despite his training and talent; the hospitals that turned him away.

"When I got to Vellore, I spent the night on the Brands' veranda, because I had nowhere else to go," said Sadan. "That was unheard of for a person with leprosy back then. I can still remember when Dr. Brand took my infected, ulcerated feet in his hands. I had been to many doctors. A few had examined my hands and feet from a distance, but Dr. Brand and his wife were the first medical workers who dared to touch me. I had nearly forgotten what human touch felt like."

Sadan then recounted the elaborate sequence of medical procedures—tendon transfers, nerve strippings, toe amputations, and cataract removal—performed by Dr. Brand and his ophthalmologist wife. He spoke for half an hour. His past life was a catalog of human suffering. But as we sipped our last cup of tea in his home, just before I left to catch a plane to England, Sadan made this astonishing statement: "Still, I must say that I am now happy that I had this disease."

"Happy?" I asked, incredulous.

"Yes," replied Sadan. "Apart from leprosy, I would have been a normal man with a normal family, chasing wealth and a higher position in society. I would never have known such wonderful people as Dr. Paul and Dr. Margaret, and I would never have known the God who lives in them."

In the later years of his practice, Dr. Brand worked on transferring the principles learned from treating leprosy patients to help those suffering from other diseases. Diabetes, for example, follows a similar pattern of insensitivity. Diabetics lose sensation in their feet, silencing the warning signals of pain; a sore develops that goes untreated; infection sets in. Just two decades ago, 100,000 diabetics per year in the U.S. were undergoing amputations because of this problem. Gradually, as the results of Dr. Brand's research became known, that trend was reversed. Dr. C. Everett Koop, former U.S. Surgeon General, claims that Dr. Brand's research has been directly responsible for eliminating the need for tens of thousands of amputations. Brand's medical practice may have ended, but his work continues to bear fruit.

After retiring from medical practice, Dr. Brand settled in Seattle. He served as president of the International Christian Medical and Dental Society, consulted with the World Health Organization and now, in his eighties, continues to lecture throughout the world.*

Over the years of our friendship, often I have felt like James Boswell, the apprentice who shadowed the great man Samuel Johnson, fervently writing down every morsel of wisdom that fell from his lips. Yet, even after three books and ten years of collaboration with Paul Brand, much had fallen through the cracks. Conversation with him tends to range over a wide field. I have corralled many of his insights and remarkable stories; many others did not fit into our three books.

God's Forever Feast [now entitled He Satisfies My Soul] pulls together some of the morsels that have not yet seen print. The title works on several levels at once, because this book represents in essence the "table talk" of Dr. Paul Brand. I have read the recorded table talk of men like Samuel Johnson, C. S. Lewis, and Martin Luther and have longed for the privilege of conversing with such great men in person. God's Forever Feast gives a sample of what I have enjoyed as a companion of Dr. Paul Brand.

You will gain from these pages a new appreciation for the freezing properties of water and a reverence for the microscopic animals in the soil and the bacteria in your colon. You'll learn about human sweat and bird-watching and "nursery logs" in the rain forests of the Pacific Northwest. And along the way,

---

* Publisher's note: Dr. Brand died on July 8, 2003, at the age of 89. Philip Yancey was one of the speakers at a memorial service celebrating Dr. Brand's life.

you'll absorb something of the spirit of a man who has permanently imprinted himself on my life.

If I had to choose one lesson I have learned from Dr. Brand, it would center on the underlying unity of life. So often in this modern world we compartmentalize. Scientists study the material world; priests and preachers study the spiritual world. Dr. Brand brings those worlds together. He sees the cosmos in a microbe, the Creator in a nerve cell. To him, the world reveals God, and God illuminates the world. For him, whether as a scientist in a laboratory, a surgeon tending to a patient, or a speaker addressing eight leprosy patients—half of whom are deaf—life is an act of worship. I know that he has only one goal for this book: to give glory to the God he loves and serves.

PHILIP YANCEY

PUBLISHER'S PREFACE
to the Third Edition

D iscovery House Publishers is pleased to bring back into print *He Satisfies My Soul*, in previous editions entitled *God's Forever Feast*. A pioneer both in medicine and in thought, Dr. Paul Brand integrated his love of the natural world with the Christian principles that informed his life from childhood. A product of this integration, *He Satisfies My Soul* provides a look at God's creation that is every bit as relevant as when this book was first published in 1993.

In this book, Dr. Brand addressed the issues that are often the subjects today of books, magazine articles, political debates, blogs, and water-cooler conversations. Intelligent design, water and soil conservation, pollution, the economy, the general protection of our environment, the temptations presented by modern media—Dr. Brand wrote about them originally in 1993 with the winsome voice of one who lived in awe of God's complex and delicate creation. His spiritual wisdom in these matters continues to speak to us now, fifteen years later.

In chapter 5, "The Good Earth," Dr. Brand wrote insightfully about his own life, almost prophetically: "My active life is behind me. Soon I will no longer occupy space. But I pray that my life and the principles that God has helped me to live by will continue to influence young lives. When we die we do not only leave seed, we also leave an effect on the soil in which future children grow and future spiritual seed will be nourished. That's one reason the psalmist says, 'Precious in the sight of the Lord is the death of his saints' (116:15). Good soil is the legacy of pioneer grasses and plants now long gone."

Dr. Brand died in 2003 at the age of 89, a few years after he penned these words. This book is only one of the many "good soil" legacies of his life, which was committed to medical science and Christian service. Our prayer is that as you read *He Satisfies My Soul*, you will wonder at the beauty of creation and the great Creator who has fashioned it all and that your soul will be nourished by the rich spiritual fruit that Dr. Brand's life and work have produced.

CHAPTER 1

And So We Thank the Lord

Many good things for us you do,
Heavenly Father we thank you.

~ OLD ENGLISH GRACE BEFORE MEALS

When he was at the table with them, he took bread,
gave thanks, broke it, and began to give it to them.
Then their eyes were opened . . .

LUKE 24:30–31

The evening newspaper in Baton Rouge, Louisiana, has a weekend magazine that ran a feature for several months titled "The Best Meal I Ever Had." Each week the editor asked Louisiana celebrities from politics or sports or entertainment to write a column about the best meal they had ever eaten, concluding with the recipes of the main courses. Eventually he ran out of celebrities and broadened his author pool to include doctors—and picked on me. This is the story I told.

We were in the Kundah Mountains of South India on holiday with four children and the Webbs, another family with four children. We vacationed together every year. We loved to hike over the hills and along the rivers, even though the youngest often needed to be carried most of the way. Both fathers enjoyed fishing, and the Billitadahalla River was full of trout.

The country was wild and desolate, and the only other humans were a boy or two keeping an eye on peaceful herds of buffalo.

For food we carried only dry bread, and for cooking, only a piece of chicken wire and a knife or two. After a stiff morning walk, we arrived at the river, and the children scattered to collect dry bits of driftwood or dead branches from the forest while the fathers selected just the right flies to bait their hooks and began to fish. Everyone knew the meal could not begin until eight or nine trout had been caught, but we didn't worry because few knew about the river and it was full of trout waiting to be caught.

Except that day.

The sky was clear and the air still. The sun was high and only the mosquitoes were active. The fish had breakfasted well and were not ready to lunch. We could see them clearly through the unruffled surface of the water, and it was obvious that they could see us. We went to our favorite pools where we usually caught our best and biggest fish. We crouched behind rocks and cast our lines until our muscles were sore. Our hooks got caught in overhanging branches, and when we reached out to catch the twigs and release the lines, we fell into the river, bruising our shins. We fished a mile or two upriver and then as far downriver. Hours passed, and the children came to inquire about the probability that lunch might be near, only to be sent back with the appalling news that not a single fish had been caught.

Lunchtime came and went. The fire burned out. The older children tried to comfort the younger ones, and the youngest was crying and chewing on the dry bread. The fathers tried to look confident but knew that their reputation as providers was rapidly being lost. This was *crisis*.

A cloud drifted over the sun. A breeze came up and ruffled the water. Suddenly both our fishing poles bent and lines became taut. We caught fish after fish and landed them on the grass. Excited, our children gathered them up and ran with them to their mothers. Relieved, the mothers split the trout and laid them on the chicken wire over the revived embers of the fire.

Wonderful smells began to drift up the river. Grilled trout were laid on slices of bread, their natural oils serving as butter. The children could scarcely wait to sing grace before biting down on the food they had doubted would ever come.

Finally we fathers arrived, carrying the final trout that would complete the meal. We were sunburned and weary with aching muscles. We were mosquito bitten, bruised, and hungry. But we were welcomed with cheers. We rested beside our families on a great rock under the shade of a twisted old tree and began to eat. We all agreed it was the best meal we had ever tasted. I, for one, still declare that it has never been bettered, not in the most expensive restaurant or by the most famous chef.

Many times since when I've been to fine restaurants, I have ordered trout, and I'm almost always disappointed. I've wanted to tell the chef I know trout can be more exciting. I even considered offering to demonstrate how to cook it myself.

It was a while before I realized my expectations were unrealistic. What my subconscious memory was seeking could never be reproduced in a kitchen. No chef has access to the essential sauce that made my special meal unique: hunger, bruises and sunburn, aching muscles, a sense of near failure transformed into success. Mix those ingredients with the happy faces of family members enjoying each other and contributing toward the shared ecstasy of grilled trout, and you have a memorable meal! (I must add that fresh grilled trout on dry bread tastes good beside any river, anywhere.)

I mentioned that the children could hardly wait to sing grace before biting down on their trout on dry bread, but wait they did, and if we parents had forgotten, the little ones would have reminded us to sing. We had a series of musical graces that each of our families used to sing before every meal. It seemed to us that they had special meaning on picnics in the open countryside. There we were surrounded with the evidence of God's bounty. On that special day we probably sang Johnny Appleseed's grace:

> The Lord is good to me,
> And so I thank the Lord,
> Who giveth me
> The things I need,
> The sun and the rain
> And the apple seed.
> The Lord is good to me.

We sometimes substituted our own words in place of "apple seed." We may have sung "The sun and the rain and the fish and the bread." Whatever the words, the music rang out from twelve voices across the river and echoed back from the hills, "And so we thank the Lord." The singing postponed the eating by just a few minutes, but I have no doubt that it enhanced the flavor of what we ate. It brought *wholeness* into each meal. The fare at our meals was not only an array of wholesome foods for our nourishment, but it also gave us a chance to be together, and it was an invitation to our Lord to take His place at the head of the table.

My family and I sang another grace before meals.

> Back of the loaf, the snowy flour,
> Back of the flour, the mill.
> Back of the mill, the grain and the shower,
> The sun, and the Father's will.

This grace gently reminds us God is the source of all that we need. He is the one who sustains and nourishes us, both physically and spiritually.

FOOD AS PARABLE

Jesus Christ was constantly using simple, down-to-earth examples from the physical realm to help His followers understand the realities of spiritual life and growth. Today, we who try to follow Him are no better equipped to understand spiritual truth than were people in Jesus' day. We, too, are mortal and finite. We, too, need to see spiritual truth in terms related to our lives.

The spiritual lessons in this book are not new, but they are, I hope, a fresh look at what the Bible teaches. The way we look at physical food and nourishment has changed significantly since Jesus' day. The use of the microscope and of modern chemistry and biology has taught us a great deal that the first disciples could never have known. This knowledge has deepened my appreciation of the aptness of the parables that Jesus chose.

My own study of life and its mechanisms for survival has increased my sense of wonder and adoration of my Lord, who made it all. Not only do the heavens proclaim His glory, but so do the seed and the soil, the trees and their fruit. God created them all. This is a book of praise for all that makes food such as bread so nourishing to our bodies. It's also a closer look at what it means to nourish our souls.

The Bible is full of meals and food. More than half of the parables of Jesus center on food or feasts or farming. I think I know why; I have only to think of the people I knew in India. Most of India still lives the way people did in Bible times. Because of the time and toil it takes to provide for the necessities of life, most people in India are still preoccupied with food.

In India the women grind whole grains of wheat at home in their own stone mill. They pound the rice in pestle and mortar to break the grains for breakfast food. They walk a mile or more with pots on their head and on their hip to draw water from the well for cooking and washing and drinking. They collect fresh spices from the farm and crush them into a paste to flavor the curry, starting after the morning meal to prepare for the evening. They pause to feed the newest baby, nursing it while they prepare gruel for the toddler. They collect firewood from the forest to have it ready for the next day's cooking. When everyone has eaten, they collect all remainders and use them to feed the chickens and the goats. They get up early to milk the goats or the family cow and take them to pasture before they start to grind the wheat for baking bread for the new day. Everything they do is related to food.

Most Americans think about food only at mealtimes. Only 5 percent of people live and work on the farm. We don't need to spend much time preparing our food. Our water comes out of a faucet, not a well. We buy our bread already baked. Much of the food we purchase is ready to heat and serve.

Mealtime tends to be buffet style. Food is grabbed from the refrigerator as we rush out the door to an activity. Many families eat in front of the television set. Food is no longer sacramental; it is simply a means to satisfy our appetite.

But even fifty years ago, things were different. A meal was more than just eating. It was a coming together of family members, an acknowledgment of God, a time to exchange news and make plans.

Attitudes toward spiritual food have changed as well. In Bible times the word *bread* conjured up images of grinding, of kneading, of baking, of harvest—of life itself. Spiritual food involved preparation and was the outworking of a person's spiritual life. Jesus, resting by the well in Samaria, turned away from the food His disciples brought Him from the town, saying, "I have had food to eat that you do not know about." He explained that His nourishment had come from doing the will of God who sent Him.

Today we go to church to receive our spiritual food. We sit in rows of chairs, as if at a meal, and expect the pastor to have prepared a feast. We may even think our spiritual food should be packaged so that we can take it on the run, with minimal interruption in our lives. However, spiritual food should not be dished out by fast food restaurants. Our spiritual food is life itself. As we put the principles of our faith into practice, we nourish our souls.

CHAPTER 2

Hunger Is the Best Sauce in the World

Hunger finds no fault with the cook.

~ C. H. SPURGEON

Blessed are you who hunger now, for you will be satisfied.

LUKE 6:21

Hunger is a wonderful thing. It gives us life. It's the body's built-in alarm that it's time to eat. Hunger is what makes eating a pleasure. Without it, we could easily forget to eat; we might even starve to death.

Most of us feel hungry when we need food, and so we think hunger is identical with our need for food. But the word *hunger* should not be used to denote an actual lack of food. The sense of need is not to be confused with the need itself. We can feel hunger when our body doesn't need food, and we can need food and yet not want it.

Hunger is simply a sense or perception of need for food. The *Oxford Dictionary* says it is "the uneasy or painful sensation caused by want of food; craving; appetite." It is a pain that demands relief. When the body needs food, the level of need is communicated to the brain as a sense.

Our senses can sometimes play tricks on us. Severe hunger is uncommon to most of us, but we've all experienced some of its early stages. We experience hunger when mealtime comes and goes and we haven't eaten. But the "hunger pains" we feel then don't indicate a real need. The body has plenty of reserves of food stored in the liver and elsewhere. We're not in danger of starvation. However, when the body is expecting a meal, it gets ready for it. The sense of hunger gets things moving. Glands in the mouth begin to secrete saliva; the stomach gets juices ready and begins to practice digestive movements. These are just stomach contractions, not real pains and not real hunger. If food is delayed further, the body accepts the situation, and the contractions wear off. They may start again when the next mealtime comes around.

People feel some hunger when the blood's sugar level falls below normal. This mild hypoglycemia happens when one has been using up sugar a little faster than it is being absorbed from the gut or when the liver is slow to release what has been stored in it. The problem corrects itself when the liver catches up. But in the meantime a person may feel hungry and take a snack "just to keep going." This compulsive response to mild hypoglycemia destroys many good diet programs designed to help a person lose weight. This feeling of hunger doesn't represent a real need for food. If a person craves food just before mealtimes and can't resist eating then, he or she should eat smaller meals and more frequently.

THE LAST HOPE OF FOOD

Children are more dependent on mealtimes and less tolerant of lack of food because they have a fast metabolism and less capacity for storage. They also have to satisfy the demands of growth. Mothers suffer when they see their children starving and often go without eating themselves in order to be able to give more to the children.

My wife, Margaret, once got a glimpse of the reactions of a child—our own child—when she was really hungry. She and our four children were in India on a journey home from a visit to my mother, Granny Brand, who lived up in the mountains. Margaret's purse had been stolen, and she was left without money for food. They still had a day's journey ahead.

She picks up the story, mid-morning: "We had no breakfast. The children entertained each other to help forget the signals from their stomachs. Then a woman boarded the train to sell a basket of small custard apples from her basket. They are about the size of small oranges, have a knobby-looking skin, and are full of shiny black seeds, each wrapped in a sweet pulp. Not much juice, but satisfying if one could just eat them slowly. I used some coins in my pocket to buy two of these fruits for each of the children. I suggested they see who could make theirs last the longest. Before any of them had finished the first one, our train drew into the station where we had to change.

"I loaded the older children with some baggage, while I picked up the rest and called to Pauline, our three-year-old youngest, to follow me as we ran to the other platform to make our connection. Suddenly I realized that Pauline was missing. Dumping my stuff, I rushed back to the stationary train where a crowd of people had gathered.

"In the middle of the group was Pauline frantically trying to guard a mess of custard apple. She had dropped it, and it had been stepped on and was smeared over the step of the train. No one could get past her. I picked her up, covered to her elbows in the remnant of her precious custard apple, and carried her, weeping, over the tracks to the others. Pauline had to stay hungry, as well as dirty and sticky, until we reached home about four hours later.

"I can still see that desperate three-year-old, separated from the remnants of her smashed custard apple, defiantly holding up her family and the whole railway system that threatened her last hope of food."

Thankfully, we in the West rarely see our children go hungry and have never known true hunger ourselves.

THE BANKERS OF THE BODY

Adults who establish a pattern of missing a meal such as lunch soon don't miss it. Their bodies adapt to the new routine. They don't salivate at the old lunchtime, and they have no hunger pains. If they miss several meals, their body uses reserves of food that have already been formed into tissues. Short-term reserves are held in the liver. Longer-term reserves are stored in fat cells, which act as bankers to the body.

In times of fasting, the fat cells give up their store and shrink. They do this a few at a time and follow a pattern based on the value of the cells to the body for various reasons other than storage.

A SOFT TOUCH

Deposits of fat can have a purpose other than storage of nutrients. They sometimes have a structural job. The kidneys, for example, are supported and cushioned by an envelope of fat that helps to protect them from injury. This fat remains undisturbed even when superficial fat cells around the abdomen and chest may be giving up their stores. Even our hands contain deposits of fat cells.

As a hand surgeon, I appreciate the fact that the little bones of each finger have collections of fat cells that lie under the skin in front of the tendons and that are firmly tied back to the bones. This gives the palm of the hand a soft and compliant feel. We enjoy shaking hands, but this habit would soon stop if when we touched each other we felt the actual bones of the skeleton just under the skin! But in God's design, fat adds gentleness to our touch. Because that fat is so important as a cushion, it remains in place, even when other fat is being used up to satisfy hunger.

Hunger at this level—when the body is just beginning to dip into its reserves—can be almost a pleasant experience. We anticipate how good the next meal is going to taste. It quickens our step as we hurry home from work. It fills our imagination with visions of rich, hot soup, and we remember good meals from the past. People who never allow themselves to become hungry never know the best joys of eating.

If hunger is allowed to go for long without the satisfaction of eating, then a gradual change takes place. The body sets up a stern system of priorities. Every system and every tissue is subjected to grading that assesses its contribution to survival. After the expendable fat cells have given up their substance, most other tissues are at risk and may have to be sacrificed to support the most vital organs.

The heart and the brain and the lungs must be maintained at all costs. The muscles and bones and connecting tissues may have to give up some of their substance to feed these really essential parts of the body.

While the body is fasting, the sense of hunger is building. This is not the hunger pain that tells you that it is time for a meal; this is a deep preoccupation with food. All else seems trivial. The sight or smell of food can turn a really hungry person into a potential thief or bandit.

OUT OF RESERVES... BANKRUPTCY!

One of the saddest sights in medical practice is kwashior-kor, a condition that was first recognized and described at a place of that name in Africa. A child in this condition has been starving for a long time and as a result has developed a severe protein deficiency.

A starving child is often fed starchy food, as that may be all that's available. Carbohydrates can keep adults going a long time, but children must have protein as well because they are growing.

The child has been hungry. All reserves of fat and muscle have been used up. The limbs are spindly, the abdomen is bloated, and the skin dry. Black hair turns reddish and dry. Hunger no longer drives the child to cry and seek for food. As death slowly approaches, apathy has replaced hunger.

I've been at the bedside of such children in India and have offered them milk and small portions of food. They just turned away and refused to eat or drink. In a hospital we can save such children by feeding them through a vein until their hunger returns. Sometimes a helper can sit beside the child, hold his reluctant mouth open, force in small amounts of food or milk, and then wait for a swallow before dripping in a little more.

The reward comes when, almost suddenly, the child looks at you and opens his own mouth for food. Appetite is coming back! A *sense* of hunger is awakening. Life will return.

Out in the villages and rural areas these children just quietly die. All fight has gone. Perhaps it is a merciful provision of the Creator that when further effort or fight has become futile, the pain of hunger is alleviated. Death comes gently, like a friend.

Kwashiorkor may be the most dramatic example of the separate identity of the sense of need and the need itself. However, there are some dangerous neurotic conditions in which people can convince themselves that they don't need food or that food is bad for them and must be vomited after it has been eaten. In fully developed anorexia nervosa and bulimia, the person, if not treated, may actually die of starvation because of a breakdown at the level of the nervous system. He or she dies of starvation without feeling hungry, even though plenty of food is available.

Researchers have conducted bizarre experiments with rats. In these experiments an electrode is implanted directly into the part of the rat's brain that registers pleasure. If the rat is given the choice of two levers, one that releases food into its dish and one that switches on direct pleasure without the need to eat, the rat presses the pleasure lever again and again until it dies of starvation. The actual need for food has been separated from the sense of need. The need for food is real, but the sense of pleasure, which is false, results in death.

A similar condition occurs in people with drug addiction. An addict on a succession of "highs" may lose awareness of many of his or her normal body needs. Many lose weight and muscle mass. Consequently, the caricature of the hollow-eyed cadaverous drug addict is sometimes not far from the truth.

AWAKENED APPETITES

What is true of the drug addicted person at a physical level is even truer at the spiritual level of large numbers of the human race. When Jesus said "Happy are they who hunger and thirst after righteousness, for they shall be filled," He was not making a distinction between those who need righteousness compared to those who don't need it. We are all in need, but we don't all know it or feel the need.

Friends and pastors may see that a person is in need of salvation and of the work of the Spirit, but there is little they can do until the person is hungry for God. We have to pray that God will awaken within this person an *appetite* for what He has to give. Then there is hope!

We have all known of devoted servants of God who have spiritually fed others by the "drip method." Mothers are often the experts in this, praying for a child who has turned away and taking every opportunity to sneak a tasty morsel of spiritual truth into conversations with the child.

Earlier, I pointed out that kwashiorkor is due to *protein* deprivation. Protein is food for growth. Just as in natural food, so in the spiritual: we must have food for growth as well as food for maintenance. Sugar and cookies are fine for immediate energy. Reading and quoting encouraging texts and promises from the Bible may help us for the moment. But for steady growth we need to read the context of these passages and realize that promises are made to specific people and types of people and that they carry conditions. Scripture calls us to action and to change the priorities in our lives. It is by meditating on these deeper realities of our faith that we begin to absorb protein from Bible study and then are able to grow.

We should never assume that the loss of spiritual appetite happens only to other people. There are times when one's own spiritual life may be at a low ebb, and the Bible seems lifeless and dull. This is not a time to stop feeding. Loss of appetite may become progressive, and even terminal, as in kwashiorkor. These are times for discipline, for forced feeding. Daily Bible reading and prayer and fellowship in God's house will tide us through.

One day your appetite will be stimulated. Words will leap out again and taste good. One day the spiritual saliva will flow again as God's Word becomes relevant to your felt need and you realize you have passed through a transient period of anorexia. The food has become as appetizing as ever.

"Some wandered in desert wastelands . . . They were hungry and thirsty, and their lives ebbed away. Then they cried out to the Lord in their trouble, and he delivered them from their distress . . . Let them give thanks to the Lord for his unfailing love and his wonderful deeds for men, for he satisfies the thirsty and fills the hungry with good things" (Psalm 107:4–9).

CHAPTER 3

Enticing Flavors,
Tantalizing Aromas

... the fruit
Of that forbidden tree whose mortal taste
Brought death unto the World, and all our woe ...

~ JOHN MILTON, *PARADISE LOST*

Taste and see that the LORD is good; blessed is the
man who takes refuge in him.

PSALM 34:8

My dear father-in-law loved to eat. He loved experiencing new flavors and tastes. That is, he did until he was in a car accident. His head struck the frame of the car, and his brain jerked forward inside his skull. His brain was unharmed, but the impact must have snapped the little nerves of smell that run up into the brain from the top of the nasal cavity. He was never able to smell anything for the rest of his life.

Poor Daddy! He never complained about not being able to smell flowers, but it was hard for him to be unable to enjoy the flavor of his meals. "Everything tastes the same," he would say. As far as he was concerned, his wife might as well not cook. He had lost his appetite and was content to have only bread at every meal.

As my father-in-law discovered, a large part of appetite is taste, and a large part of taste is aroma. Good cooks know that even a jaded appetite can be aroused. Tantalizing aromas can awaken a person's desire for sustenance and help make eating pleasurable.

Our Creator designed the human body in such a way that it doesn't need to carry much food and fuel in storage. He gave us hunger to prompt us to eat when stocks became low, but He also made eating a pleasure so we would want to do what we had to do. The aroma draws us to the food, and taste satisfies when we put the food into our mouth.

Just as it's possible to awaken someone's physical appetite, so it is with the spiritual appetite. God calls you and me to be fragrant aromas of Him and to entice others to "taste of the goodness of the Lord." In order to understand how we can do this, let's take a closer look at the way taste and smell arouse the appetite and linger in the memory.

Because taste and smell are linked, we often confuse the two. When we put food into our mouth, we sense a wide range of flavors, and we call it taste. But in fact, most of what we call taste is really smell. The nerves of taste run to the brain from little pits in the mouth and tongue that are called taste buds. These tiny sense organs are big enough to see with the naked eye. They look like little buds on the surface of the tongue, mostly near the edges. Careful tests have shown that taste buds can identify only a few tastes. They can recognize *sweet* and *sour, acid, bitter,* and *salt,* and mixtures of any of these five.

All the other hundreds of flavors we taste are actually aromas we smell. When we eat, the aromas drift up behind our soft palate into our nasal cavity, where the nerves of smell end in little cells (olfactory cells), some of the most amazing chemical laboratories on earth. These smell organs tell us the flavor of our food. If you find that difficult to believe, think about it next time you have a heavy cold. If your sinuses and nasal cavity are blocked, you'll find that you can't taste your food any more or will be able to taste only salt and sweet, bitter (as in quinine), acid (as in lemon), and sour. In other words, if your nose is blocked, don't spend your money on a gourmet meal.

THE NOSE KNOWS

Most of us don't appreciate many parts of the body until we lose them. I learned, however, to appreciate the marvels of smell and taste when as a medical student I had to work as an analytical chemist for a few weeks. My classmates and I had to analyze single, simple substances that were in a solution, such as magnesium sulfate in water. We knew how to pour known acids into the same test tube and see how the unknown substance changed color. We used litmus paper, and other prepared tests, and soon came up triumphantly with an answer. Then we went on to analyze mixtures of two or three simple substances. For that we needed a shelf of bottles of standard chemicals for our tests. The bottles had to have clear labels in order for us to know what testing reagents we were using.

Finally, we had to analyze and identify organic chemicals, the kind of things that are the building blocks of living plants and animals. My classmates and I never got far because these chemicals are complex. There are long chains of amino acids and sugars, and it isn't enough to know that a certain sugar is there. It's essential to know just where it is in a chain of other substances. If the links in a chain are in a different order, the substance may function quite differently. This was beyond our knowledge and skill and beyond ordinary laboratories, too. Specialists may take days working on a single organic substance before they can tell exactly what it is.

As students, we usually had a test tube full of the stuff we had to test. A good chemist would do it with less, perhaps a cubic centimeter to work with, so he could use one drop for each of the many tests to be done. If he had to identify a mixture of two or more organic substances by chemical tests, it might take weeks. He'd need a good supply of the mixture.

The olfactory cells in our noses function as chemical laboratories that analyze real organic chemicals. The nose receives an unknown mixture of minute quantities of strange substances and then has to chemically analyze each of them and then report the result to the brain in a language the brain can understand. The nose doesn't need a cubic centimeter of coriander or garlic or human sweat to identify the aroma. Put one- thousandth of a drop in front of my face, a speck too small to see or to weigh, and my nose would take one breath and say "Ah! Cloves!" or "Human sweat!"

At the end of a day in the chemical laboratory, I used to go home and enter the front door. Immediately, without conscious thought or analysis, I would often know what was for dinner. That knowledge came from the analysis inside my nose of microscopic specks of the actual substance of the soup or bacon that had escaped in the steam from the cooking pot in the kitchen. The information from my nose had been coded into nerve signals and sent to my brain, where it was decoded and then matched with memories of smells from previous meals. My brain didn't receive the information in technical terms. It came simply as knowledge, compared with memory—immediate and sure.

People who live in industrialized societies have usually neglected their sense of smell. African tribesmen can identify aromas much better, and many animals better still. A moth can recognize the sex smell of another moth a mile away and will find its mate by flying upwind so long as it can pick up a single molecule of that scent every hundred yards or so. A bloodhound, given a sock to smell, will track the person who wore that sock through miles of field and forest, even though the scent is a day old. Yet the only clue is an occasional submicroscopic speck of the actual substance of that man or his sweat that lingers in the air near the ground he has walked on, wearing a different pair of socks!

The actual chemical make-up of sweat is much the same for all humans, and a good chemist should be able to identify sweat within a few hours if he or she had enough of it to work with. No chemist on earth could tell the sweat of one man from the sweat of his brother, even if given a million molecules to work with. The nose of the dog, sniffing one molecule among thousands of others in the forest, can say in a moment, "That is the man."

THE REMBRANDTS OF THE BODY

My nose is not as good as that of some animals, but my sense of taste and smell must still be rated as the chemical masterpieces of my body. The analytical cells in the nose give instant answers to questions about the nature of the environment and the safety of food. These cells are then linked to a most remarkable network of nerves in the brain called the limbic system, of which the rhinencephalon, or smell-brain, is an important part. This section of the brain looks large for what we may think of as a small function. It is not a small function. It needs a lot of brain partly because the chemistry of the olfactory cells in the nose needs a lot of analysis at the brain level as well as at the level of the chemical detectors. It is also because smell is linked at many levels to memory and experience.

When I arrive in India each year, my mind is full of plans and ideas about where I want to go and what I hope to do.

When I step off the plane and take my first breath, all of India rushes into my being. My relationship with India changes; in a moment India becomes real. It has substance. As I walk along the street in the open bazaar, I am a child again; a doctor; a father with my children. I can shut my eyes, but the reality does not disappear. It has entered through my nose. The aromas of cattle, cow dung, incense, and sandalwood have all been imprinted in my subconscious mind seventy years ago and renewed and reinforced year by year. Every year I think about India on my way there, but it's a memory and a dream until I breathe it fresh and open the nerve gates to hidden and forgotten experiences of long ago.

No wonder the hippocampus is big! It has a number of tasks, each extraordinary. First, it must change a purely chemical analysis in the nose into a series of nerve impulses that are electronic and mathematical in nature. It is a code of chemistry. Then it must recognize and decode the nerve impulses that identify the substance smelled. Only important and significant smells are transmitted to the consciousness for thought and reflection. Finally the hippocampus records the memory of each smell and keeps it in association with the findings of other senses and events and experiences. All of this is available at a moment's notice when we smell something similar. We will perceive danger or pleasure because of the experiences associated with when it happened before.

Certain aromas can cause us to remember great meals we have tasted. Today, in Washington State, when I taste south Indian hot curry, I am back as a three- or four-year-old in the wooden bungalow with my parents and baby sister. I have wakened from sleep and climbed out of bed from under the mosquito net. I step into the living room and see Mother and Dad at the table with an oil lamp between them. Mother is taking a spoonful of curry directly from the dish and slurping it into her mouth with obvious relish. She turns to look at me with the spoon still at her lips. I forget why I have come to her because the curry smells different from what I have had before, and I ask for some. Mother says it is too hot for me. When I am a little older she will let me have the stronger spices. I probably cry, but anyway she gives me a taste, and I go back to bed with a mildly burning mouth and a sense that growing up had better come soon, if it brings tastes like that.

That little cameo of memory is unique. I don't remember other things from that period of my childhood. Those few minutes are clear in every detail and are brought to mind by taste and smell.

I am thankful that my parents and foster parents always insisted that I eat everything on my plate. If a flavor was new, and I didn't like it, I was given just a little, but it had to be eaten because one day I would get to like it. I now enjoy a wide range of food and am not bothered by a lot of hang-ups.

When I go to a new country, I determine not to ask for American food. I reckon that Burmese cooks know how to cook Burmese food, and Ethiopian cooks do a good job with Ethiopian food. They may have no idea of the finer points of American dishes and may ruin them. The fact that Thailanders enjoy Thai food proves that to enjoy it needs only practice and an open mind. Food is a social affair as well as a matter of nourishment, and friendships are often sealed over mealtimes, especially if there is mutual appreciation of food prepared in the home or a local eating place.

Just as there is a discipline about taste, there is also a discipline about the atmosphere in which food is eaten. In a family where discipline is elevated to a higher plane than love, children may resent having to come to meals and may develop lasting dislike for foods they may be forced to eat. On the other hand, children really do get to like and enjoy the foods they are encouraged to eat, and an atmosphere of appreciation enhances taste. If a young child is allowed to express disgust at table, that attitude becomes imprinted on the taste image of that food and makes it more difficult to like it later in life. It also affects the enjoyment of everyone else eating the food that has been vilified. Mealtimes are a wonderful opportunity for the exercise of all the skills of parenthood. Love is the first, and discipline the second, and they are not incompatible.

THE INTIMACY OF TASTE

In the Bible both taste and smell are used to indicate appreciation for something. Throughout Exodus and Leviticus, burnt offerings and sacrifices are referred to as producing a "sweet savor," or sweet smell, to the Lord. The apostle Paul in 2 Corinthians 2:15–16 speaks of our being the aroma of Christ to God. He then says we smell of death to those who are perishing but are the fragrance of life to those being saved.

David wrote a psalm of 176 verses (Psalm 119), each of which expressed gratitude for the Word of God. In verse 103 he uses taste: "How sweet are your words to my taste, sweeter than honey to my mouth!" Taste includes smell but is more intimate. We can't know God entirely by the distant senses of sight and hearing. We have to receive Him into ourselves before we can know His sweetness. His aroma may tantalize, but taste involves an intimate commitment to Him.

Few cities in the world have the variety of ethnic restaurants found in London, England, where I did my medical training. It was only a short walk from my hospital to a street full of Greek, Japanese, and other European and Asian eating places. At the end of a heavy day of operations, my chief would suggest to his two assistants that we all go out to eat. We rarely had plans of where to go. We just walked down that street. Before long an aroma would invite us in, and we would relax over the delight of some new delicate taste.

That street represents to me the variety of delights that are to be enjoyed from God's good earth. The flavors and aromas are skillfully blended and extracted from a number of herbs and plants that have grown for centuries in particular parts of the world. The adventurous ones who first explored the range of tastes shared what they had found. Now we can try them for ourselves.

The same is true of spiritual food: delights abound for all of us. We have to believe that spiritual nutrients are there and then seek them out and taste and see if they are good.

We are invited to receive the person of the Spirit of God into our inner being. We are invited to *taste* and enjoy Him. How close, how intimate is taste! We actually savor God. And He not only accepts our flavor when He takes us into himself but delights in the aroma of the sacrifice—the commitment of our lives to Him.

The Old Testament frequently refers to God's enjoyment of the sweet aroma of the sacrifices offered to Him. In fact, from the mention of Noah's sacrifice after the flood until the end of Leviticus, there are forty times when it states that the offering was a sweet aroma to the Lord. Undoubtedly the phrase was symbolic and represented that aspect of the sacrifice that was enjoyed by all the people who smelled it and who saw the fragrant smoke rising upward, symbolizing the gift of their best to God.

HOW DO YOU TASTE WORSHIP?

In all the oldest traditions of the church, the use of taste and aroma are prominent, and incense is still a regular part of worship in many churches. Children who are taken to such churches as infants have a lasting sensory link with the atmosphere of church. Like the solemn sounds of sacred music, the fragrance of the incense and the taste of the bread and wine are all symbolic of the sensory harmony and reverence and joy of the things that God and we can enjoy together.

I grew up in a church tradition that looked upon incense and vestments and candles as almost idolatrous because they focused the mind on palpable things that might take the place of the purely spiritual. Yet as long as we recognize the incense for what it is—a symbol of the fragrance that Christ imparts to His church by His sacrifice and the sweet savor of the giving of ourselves as living sacrifices back to Him—then it may be a good use of our physical senses to remind us of spiritual truth.

A FRAGRANCE OF LIFE ... OR DEATH?

When I was about ten years old, having been exposed for the first time to all the cold and flu germs at school in England, I developed large tonsils and adenoids. I was admitted to the hospital to have them removed. I had met the surgeon who was to do the operation but didn't meet the anesthesiologist until I was in the operating room. He spoke kindly and told me I would just smell a sweet aroma and then would fall asleep. He then lowered a mask over my nose and mouth, and suddenly I found myself breathing a strong, stifling smell that seemed to choke me.

I panicked! I thought the anesthesiologist had lied to me, and therefore he must be a wicked man. I feared the operation was just a plot to kill me and that my family had been kept away so they could not protect me. I believed I was on my own against this gang of assassins. I had to fight for my life. And fight I did. I was a strong kid, and I reared up on the table and struck the doctor in the face with my fist. I tried to climb off the table but was held by a belt. Nurses and orderlies were called in, and I was finally held down while the suffocating ether took its effect.

I drifted back into consciousness in my hospital bed with a sore throat and a fear and hatred of the smell of ether that has lasted most of my life. To me ether is the smell of death. I never saw the anesthesiologist again. I rather hope he suffered a black eye or other bruises. He deserved them, for he never should have been allowed to treat a young child. If he had told me ahead of time that ether had a strong and suffocating smell but that I would soon fall asleep, then I am sure I would have tried to cooperate.

Because of my own experience as a patient, when I became a doctor I took special care in winning the confidence of my patients before taking them to the operating room and giving them ether. I told them about its strong smell but that after a few breaths they would fall asleep. I was using the vapor that had terrified me, but I had taught them to be grateful to it because it prevented them from feeling the pain of the surgery.

Paul says, "We are to God the aroma of Christ among those who are being saved and those who are perishing. To the one we are the smell of death; to the other, the fragrance of life" (2 Corinthians 2:15–16).

We are to carry the aroma of Christ to the world. It is a life-giving essence of all that Christ means to us and can mean to others. We have the responsibility of passing it on. The way we do it is of critical importance. The apostle felt the responsibility was severe. "Who is equal to such a task?" he asks. It is true that people have been turned away from the gospel by the behavior of those who profess the name and aroma of Christ. We need to be faithful carriers of the fragrance, lest it become for some the smell of death.

Great chefs spend time and skill devising better ways to present food. Doubtless part of their effort is simply to make food nourishing and easy to digest. The greatest cooks gain their reputation by the way they blend flavor and aroma so that the food becomes enticing. Should we, who represent our Lord to the people around us, be any less concerned with making our message attractive?

When people are near us, the fragrance of our lives should make their mouths water. Many Christians feel the need to be confrontational, as though they wanted to challenge a person to taste what they have. "Eat that if your stomach is strong enough!" Others may be too shy to believe that their gospel is really tempting. The life of the Spirit, lived out with simplicity and sincerity, is a sweet savor, not only to God but to observers around us. Take off the lid, and let the aroma be a message!

CHAPTER 4

The Ultimate Thirst Quencher

Whoever is thirsty, let him come; and whoever wishes,
let him take the free gift of the water of life.

REVELATION 22:17

If anyone gives even a cup of cold water to one of
these little ones because he is my disciple, . . . he will
certainly not lose his reward.

MATTHEW 10:42

I have often flown over the Middle East from Ethiopia to
Italy on my way home from Addis Ababa. It's a dreary flight,
depressing for one who loves God's earth. The view from the
window is desert, desert, and more desert. Then, all of a sudden, the scene changes. The land below is green. We fly over
fields and orchards. We can see the thread of the Jordan River
and the fertile slopes of the Golan Heights. We're flying over
Israel.

The story of the greening of Israel is the story of hard work
and water. For Israel, water is life. Jewish settlers from all over
the world came with enthusiasm to restore a land that they
believed was God's gift to them. Many came with advanced
understanding of how to make a land fertile. The river Jordan

and tributaries provided the water. It was pumped up and out to where it was distributed and used with strict conservation. Water was and is the lifeblood of Israel, and it is treated as such. So the land has become green.

The people of India, who have battled numerous droughts, also know the life-giving properties of water. Daily, Indian women walk to the well with one water pot on their head and another on their hip, only to wait their turn at the well. They let down a bucket on a rope over the pulley and haul it up two or three times till they fill their pots.

In a drought the village people watch the level of water dropping lower and lower until there is only a pool at the bottom renewed by a thin trickle. It provides just enough water for the few women who get to the well first. When the well is dry, they migrate to find a well with a better supply. Sometimes fighting breaks out as villagers defend their well from other water seekers. These people are fighting for their life.

Water is the universal medium of life. Without water, our fields would dry up, and we would have no nourishment. Without water no cell in our body could survive. Even our bones need water. Without water all of life would perish.

JUST WHAT THE DOCTOR ORDERED

One of the numerous evidences of design and purpose in the creation of life is the nature of water itself. Those who maintain that everything in the universe "just happened" are at a loss to explain how it is that water contains exactly what life needs for survival.

Almost all elements in the universe have physical features in common. All exist in various states, such as solid, liquid, and gas. They move from one physical state to another on the basis of temperature and pressure. At low temperatures they are solid, and as the temperature rises they liquefy. As temperatures continue to rise, they turn to gas. Similarly, as pressure becomes lower, substances change from solid to liquid and then to gas.

When solids become liquids, they increase in volume, and when liquids become gas, they occupy even more space. This is true for all the elements except water. Water is the only rebel.

Water obeys all the standard laws while it is a vapor. As the temperature falls, it still obeys the laws while it becomes a liquid and while liquid water cools. Its volume becomes smaller as temperature becomes lower, until it reaches four degrees Celsius. Then suddenly, as the temperature falls to three degrees and then two and one, water stops shrinking and starts to swell. Its volume rises instead of falls. At zero degrees Celsius water becomes ice, but its volume becomes larger, not smaller. This is quite extraordinary. There is no explanation for such an aberration unless it's seen as a deliberate change in the laws of physics designed to promote life.

Let me explain. Ice floats on water. Every other substance sinks when it changes from liquid to solid. If ice were to sink, oceans and lakes would become frozen from the bottom up in winter and be solid ice before the thaw. The warming effect of the sun in summer would never affect the mass of ocean ice. Ice would eternally fill the oceans and lakes. Fish and plant life could not survive. But since ice floats, it forms a crust that thickens as it gets colder. Deep water underneath is protected and stays fluid. Fish can swim and stay alive until their frozen roof is lifted and the thaw opens them again to the sky.

I first learned about the way water freezes while I was a child at school in London. It was winter, and our pipes at home had frozen. My physics teacher joked as he explained that the pipes burst because water expands when it freezes. He said it was "lucky" that water expanded when frozen because otherwise the fish would die.

After school I walked home across nearby Hampstead Heath, where nature was still wild. I used to feed the ducks, but that day I took a stone and broke the ice on a pond. I dropped crumbs into the water and saw little fish take them at the surface. They were very much alive. I don't suppose I had any profound thoughts about God or creation, but I did think my teacher's word "lucky" was very much an understatement about the wonder of water.

Water has another serendipitous quality: it replenishes and cleanses itself. Water evaporates to become a vapor and condenses back to water again. Water runs down from highlands to lowlands, dissolving salt and minerals, which are then deposited in the sea. The sea becomes saturated with earth salts of various kinds. These aren't poisonous, but they diminish the use of the water for further solvent activity in the chemistry of plant and human life. However, when water evaporates, fresh water vapor is extracted from the oceans and blown around the earth as clouds, returning fresh water to land as rain. A constant circulation of fresh water is made available.

A cup of cold water is a product of special laws of physics and hydraulics around which are twined the laws of biology. It comes from root systems that seem to know how to trap water in its headlong rush from sky to ocean and hold it long enough to satisfy their own needs with plenty left over for animals and humans to use. How could anyone believe that such a complex and ideal system could have "just happened"?

A PRICELESS SPONGE

Water is also mobile. It runs. It streams downhill over rocks and through sand until it joins other streams and rushes to the sea. Left unchecked, water can be destructive. In heavy rain, torrents of water tear up rocks and stones and cut deep channels and ravines. Crops are torn away and hurry to the sea.

But God has designed the world so that most water is tamed and is used to build and sustain life. When it rains, water falls on lichens, mosses, grasses, and plants and trees. A tangle of roots grows and forms a network around grains of soil. The soil holds the water like a sponge until the moist earth has had enough.

The water then leaves at leisure. There is a long, slow pause between rapid rain and rapid stream. It is in that pause that life prospers and grows.

There are other mechanisms by which fresh water is stored for later use. Often due to the haphazard movements of tectonic plates and earthquakes and glaciers, fresh water sometimes accumulates as lakes if there are no slopes for rivers to run downhill.

Underground lakes, known as aquifers, also store water. Fresh water, flowing over certain types of rock, finds crevices and pathways to seep down and form great reservoirs beneath the ground. Most of these vast collections have formed over centuries. During droughts farmers often dig wells and tap into aquifers to irrigate their land.

God designed our bodies so that water is critical for our survival, but He also created a universe that, if well-tended, will automatically provide all the water we need.

Just outside Darwin, Australia, an old Jeep stands on the road going south beside the signpost that points across the great desert to Alice Springs. In the driver's seat is a human skeleton with his arms on the steering wheel. A notice over his skull says, "Do you have enough water? There is no more until Alice Springs. Do you have gasoline? No more filling stations." They say the skeleton and the Jeep were found together in the desert with no gasoline in the tank and no water in the flask.

Without water, we die.

Just as hunger is a compulsion that makes it impossible to ignore our bodies' need for nourishment, thirst makes it impossible for us to forget our need for water. Thirst, the sensation that stimulates us to drink fluids, is a life-giving compulsion. Thirst sustains life. It begins with the sense that a drink would be nice and refreshing. It becomes a mild discomfort that prompts us to stop and get a drink. If the need is ignored, the discomfort grows until it forces us to go and seek water at any cost. As the desert traveler who has gone days without water knows, thirst can become our sole preoccupation. God created us so that our bodies don't let us forget our need to drink. When we go without water, we long to have our thirst quenched.

AS THE DEER PANTS FOR WATER

"Come, all you who are thirsty, come to the waters" (Isaiah 55:1). The psalmist likens his thirst for God to the need of the hunted deer, running from the dogs and panting for the water brooks (Psalm 42:1). This is a vivid scene of conflicting priorities, each related to survival. The deer is running for her life. She hears the baying of the hounds and knows the hunters are not far behind. She feels the pounding of her heart and strains her chest and lungs to their limits.

Her body is using more and more moisture; her tongue, hanging out to cool the fever of her body, is dry. Her throat is swelling, and breathing is becoming harsh.

Finally, every cell in the body cries out for the water which is life, and the deer swerves off course for the stream of water at which she absolutely must drink. She may lose her life at the hand of the hunter because she must save it by slaking her thirst.

What a powerful image! "As the deer . . . so my soul. . . ." David penned this image at a low moment in his life. He was in danger from his enemies and depressed that God seemed silent. His soul—not his body—cries out in thirst for God. This is a picture of modern man. Having sought satisfaction at every physical level, we become aware of a rising sense of need, an emptiness. Happy are those who recognize that what we long for is God and that He alone can bring the satisfaction we so desperately seek.

Our soul needs the Spirit of God! The deer risks death in the quest to quench its thirst. Jesus says, "Whoever wants to save his life will lose it, but whoever loses his life for me will find it. What good will it be for a man if he gains the whole world, yet forfeits his soul?" (Matthew 16:25).

In John 7:37–38 we have an account of one of the most powerful calls that came from Jesus: "On the last and greatest day of the Feast, Jesus stood and said in a loud voice, 'If anyone is thirsty, let him come to me and drink. Whoever believes in me, as the Scripture has said, streams of living water will flow from within him.'"

As Jesus knew, the images of thirst and living water stimulate an awareness of need in the hearts of those who have lived without God. Just as water is the medium in which all the chemistry of the physical body takes place, so the Holy Spirit is the medium of all spiritual activity. When men and women try to live a good life while denying their dependence on God, there is a deep frustration and a dryness. The cry "If you are thirsty, come to me and drink" arouses a strong surge of self-recognition that says, "Yes! That's me!"

David Brainerd, great preacher and missionary to the Indian tribes in New York, New Jersey, and eastern Pennsylvania in the eighteenth century, discovered how powerful this image was early in his ministry. One day in 1774, David, discouraged and sick, set aside a day for fasting and prayer. During that time he sensed the presence of the Spirit of God inviting him to come and drink. This reminded David of the words of Jesus in John 7 promising not only water for his own thirst but "rivers of water flowing out of him."

Following that prayer David went out and preached with power, using that same text and appeal, time after time. He came to realize how many thirsty people there are and how wonderfully God uses His own words to awaken them to their need for Him. Like David Brainerd, we need to respond to the call of Jesus and allow Him to be the water of life to us, to fill our deepest needs. Then we shall experience the bonus: others will quench their thirst from the rivers flowing out of us. The source is God himself.

BORN WITH A THIRST-METER

Our bodies have a built-in trigger, a gauge, which alerts us to our need for water: thirst. It is extraordinary to me how accurate our sense of thirst is. It is much superior to modern technology and science.

When I was a surgeon at the Christian Medical College in India, I often had to take out a badly ulcerated stomach and make new pathways for the food. During and after an operation we could not allow patients to eat or drink because the stomach and intestines had to be at rest so they could heal. All fluids had to be given intravenously. The responsibility for monitoring the patient's intake of fluids rested with the hospital staff. If we gave too little fluid, the patient would become dehydrated and wouldn't heal well. If we gave too much, the overloaded bloodstream might overflow into the lungs, causing the patient to begin to drown.

We had the nurses keep accurate records of all fluids that went in and out of the body. Every bottle of fluid was recorded on the "in" side, and every drop of urine had to be measured and recorded on the "out" side. We were relentless in our pursuit of accuracy. We estimated how much was lost by sweating and even recorded the sips of water used to moisten the mouth.

When I would make rounds, I listened to the sound of a patient's breathing through my stethoscope. If I heard bubbles, I would ask the nurses, "Are you sure you are not putting in too much fluid?" We would add up the figures again and probably slow down the rate of flow of the intravenous fluid.

We would follow this procedure until one day I'd say, "I think the stomach has healed enough now. Let's take out the needle, disconnect the bottle, and let him take fluids by mouth whenever he feels thirsty." Everyone would sigh with relief. All our advanced technology would be thrown away, and we would stop worrying. Why? Because now the patient was in charge. The poor illiterate villager who knew no science and had never been to school was far better equipped to keep his fluid balance than all of us scientists in the big hospital. He had been born with a thirst-meter inside.

NOT A DROP WASTED

Not only did God create us with a reliable and wonderful thirst-meter, He also gave us a remarkable water conservation system. Every time we eat a meal, our body pours a huge volume of water into our intestines to carry all the digestive juices and to turn all the solid food we have eaten into a thin soup. A lot of that fluid is taken back into the body while the food is absorbed. The rest is absorbed from the feces in the lower bowel. Almost none is lost. It is ready to be poured out again when the next meal comes down.

The kidneys are the perfect water conservation system. Their job is to get rid of the urea and other end products of our metabolism that would poison us if left to accumulate. The kidneys are beautifully designed organs. Every drop of blood in our body visits a kidney every few minutes. On each visit the blood passes through an exquisite little tuft of capillaries with walls so thin that fluid leaks out into tubules that surround them. The fabric of the capillaries is like a web, with holes that let small molecules through but hold back big molecules like protein and all the red and white cells. That fluid that leaks out contains all the small molecules, including residues we need to get rid of, but also a lot of chemical compounds, such as sugar, that the body needs.

So, having filtered out a lot of water with a load of dissolved solids, the tubules carry the mixture through a series of convoluted tubes that act as reverse filters. These tubes suck back into the bloodstream just those chemicals and sugars that we need to keep, together with most of the water, leaving only excess water and unneeded solids to go on to the bladder and be passed out as urine.

But, for this process to work efficiently, there must be enough water to keep all the solids in solution. When the body is short of water, the kidneys can't function properly, and there is danger of kidney stones forming. I almost learned this first-hand.

When I arrived in India, I spent the greater part of every day in the operating rooms. I was one of only two qualified surgeons in a big hospital. There was no air conditioning, and the roofs were flat and exposed to the blazing sun of the summer. I sweated so much that I soaked my scrub suits and gowns and had to change between every long operation. Sometimes my clothes were wringing wet. I was thirsty and would drink pints of water between surgeries.

As a result of the constant sweating, I developed "prickly heat," an irritating skin rash that is common in hot climates. I wanted to scratch all over my body, but in my sterile surgical gown and gloves, scratching was impossible. I just had to grit my teeth and bear it. Someone told me the rash would go away if I didn't drink so much. I would sweat less. I tried that, and it was true. The prickly heat cleared up.

Soon after, Dr. Somervell, an older missionary surgeon, came to visit. I told him the saga of my sweating problems. He gave me his advice: "You have a choice. In this weather, you can have prickly heat, or you can have kidney stones—one or the other." He went on, "When I first came to India, I did just what you have done. My prickly heat cleared up when I stopped drinking so much, but then I noticed that I was passing small amounts of concentrated urine. The next thing I knew, I had developed kidney stones because I was not taking enough water to keep the urea dissolved. It crystallized out as stones. You must trust your instinct to drink. It is your defense against having stones in your kidney."

I made my choice: I drank more. The prickly heat returned, but I was passing more urine, and I never had kidney stones!

A CONTINUOUS SUPPLY

Just as our bodies need a constant supply of water in order to function properly, so our spirits need the water of life for cleansing and for growth. The fifty-fifth chapter of Isaiah begins with a call to everyone who is thirsty to come to the water and then goes on to use the rain and snow as a picture of the way God's Word goes out over the earth to promote growth of new life. "As the rain cometh down, and the snow from heaven, and returneth not thither, but watereth the earth, and maketh it bring forth and bud, that it may give seed to the sower, and bread to the eater: So shall my word be that goeth forth out of my mouth: it shall not return unto me void, but it shall accomplish that which I please, and it shall prosper in the thing whereto I sent it" (Isaiah 55:10–11 KJV).

The Bible often uses the metaphor of a river to symbolize continuity of life and fruitfulness. The life and the grace of God need to be our constant and continual supply. Rain is temporary and sporadic, but rivers are continuous. Psalm 1 and Jeremiah 17 both call us to be like a tree planted by the rivers of water, bringing forth fruit at every season. What an inspiring goal—not only to receive the living Word of God and to have a continuous supply of it, but also to become a continuous supply of the fruit to others!

The people of Israel knew about desert experiences and the challenge of having a continuous supply of water. They had wandered in a desert for forty years and were familiar with its fruit.

Desert travelers are always on the lookout for palm trees. After miles of unrelieved sand, the sight of a distant clump of date palms can mean fruit and an oasis. That is a good place to camp, to wash and drink, and to refill stocks of water and dates.

As Christians it is wise for us to realize that desert experiences may happen to anybody. One just has to be prepared. There are times when it is not easy to find and enjoy nourishment from the Word. We feel thirst but are unable to find relief.

In such times, we need to ask God to quench our thirst. Moses prayed for water in the desert for the people he led, and God caused water to flow from under a rock.

Water tastes all the more sweet if we have to dig for it through the sand of an oasis. The same sand that makes the desert is also a great filter. We have to work for it, but it satisfies.

SQUANDERING OUR LIFE SOURCE

Besides preparing for spiritual desert experiences, we need to be good stewards of God's generous provision of what we need to sustain life. Today greed is threatening God's provision. We are depleting our water supply. We are squandering our life source.

As people have multiplied, competition for fresh water has increased. In the state of Texas, for example, the rainfall was not enough to grow food for everyone and for the great herds of cattle. Texans discovered that their state was sitting on one of the greatest aquifers in the world. The Ogallala Aquifer could supply farms and people for hundreds of years—if it was used in moderation. But each farmer and each industrialist wanted more.

They drilled deeper wells and still deeper wells, and the water level fell lower and lower. For the last several years, the water level in the Ogallala Aquifer has fallen six inches every year. That means fifty feet each century! More and more farms in Texas have to give up irrigation because it has become too expensive to pump up the water. Thirty percent of all irrigated farmland in Texas has gone out of production for this reason since 1975, and this trend will continue. Texas is going dry. The same story could be told about much of the best farmland in the world.

In my own beloved Tamil Nadu in South India, where our family all grew up, the water table has fallen ninety feet in a decade. This has meant the drying up of most of the old-style agricultural wells, where oxen were used to lift water twenty or thirty feet to the rice fields. Now, in many areas, only deep drilling can reach water, and only the rich can afford the pumps. The energy of oxen came from hay and stubble. The electric energy for pumps does not use hay; it makes the rural area more dependent on petroleum and merely pushes the day of real famine up a few years till oil runs out.

BLOWING A WHISTLE ON THE RACE

With today's water crisis, brought about by overuse and pollution and waste, the church has a responsibility. We should be leading the way, demonstrating by our own lives the joy of frugality and simplicity of lifestyle. We can also lead the way in calling people together to look ahead. We can influence local governments to halt the race to use up all our natural resources and urge them to plan the fair distribution of water. The churches of North Carolina are to be commended for doing just that. They have gotten together and formed the Land Stewardship Council of North Carolina. This Christian organization has had a real impact on the policies of the state with regard to farmland and forests, and thus to water.

Not only are we depleting our water supply, we are also spoiling it. When my wife and I left India, we moved to Louisiana and lived for the next several years on the banks of the Mississippi. That historic river, which drains most of the central area of the United States, was only a hundred yards from our front door. I began to inquire about the price of sailboats so we could enjoy our river. I was quickly warned that the river was so polluted that people who fell in were usually taken to the hospital to have their stomachs pumped out.

Our river has been nicknamed the Big Muddy. It has carried mud from thousands of farms—soil from Iowa, Kansas, Ohio, and many other farm states. With the soil, it has carried agricultural pesticides and sewage from the towns upriver. Worst of all it has transported toxic chemical wastes from industries that found it a cheap way to dispose of their effluents. It was sad to walk along a river bank and see no frogs. What had once been water of life was now a river of death.

Efforts are now under way to clean up the river. It can be done! At one time there were salmon in the Thames River in Britain. By the time I, as a child, knew it, it had become so polluted that most self-respecting fish refused to live there. Through a great effort, the sources of pollution have been identified, and by the application of rules to towns and farms and industries upriver, the Thames is fit to swim in again, and I'm told that the salmon are back!

Clean water for our good earth is the responsibility of everyone, especially those who believe God is the creator and sustainer of life. We know human nature is depraved. We know greed is endemic. Some of the most toxic pollutants are hard to detect and make no smell. God's good gifts are being spoiled. As members of the human race, we share responsibility. As Christians, we must seek God's guidance as to how we can help to renew the earth.

CHAPTER 5

The Good Earth

———

The Lord God formed the man from the dust of the
ground and breathed into his nostrils the breath of life,
and the man became a living being.

GENESIS 2:7

Dust you are and to dust you will return.

GENESIS 3:19

I remember sitting with my mother on the steps of the guest
house at a leprosy hospital in India. We were facing east,
and the sun was rising over the mountains opposite us, flooding us with early light. I was soon to leave India, and Mother
had a prophetic sense that she would not see me again. At
ninety-five, Mother knew she would not live much longer and
was giving me instructions about the way she wanted to be
buried: "Don't let them make a coffin for me," she pleaded.
"Too many trees are being cut down on the hills. There's no
sense in making a box for me to be buried in. It is just a waste
of wood. Tell them to wrap me in an old sheet—not a new
one—and let them scatter flowers over my body before they
lower me into the ground.

"I know they will want to cry, because they love me. But tell them to choose joyful hymns to sing and hymns of victory. It's not me that they will be burying, but just my old body. I am going to be with my Lord. I may even be able to see them singing. I shall not be crying and will not regret to see my body return to the earth. It has been a good body, but it has been getting weak and stiff lately, and it is time to put it away."

I couldn't reply. We just sat together, holding hands, until the sun became too hot for comfort. We went indoors and had breakfast, and I left the hospital, never to see her again. A month or two later she died. It fell to my beloved student and fellow worker, Dr. Ernest Fritschi, to fulfill the functions of a son and take my mother's body up to the mountains and to preside over the arrangements for her burial.

There is something triumphant about the death of a saint. Dust to dust—yes, but also spirit leaping up to report to God about the completion of the great adventure by which one or two hundred pounds of mud have been inspired—inbreathed—to be active and creative in God's service. That transformed mud and clay body has been the messenger of God and the instrument of His love for many years.

Hallelujah! God has done it again! He has allowed a mass of lifeless earth to come to life and live and breathe and think and love for years and years of creative activity.

I have returned to the church that my father and mother built on those mountains and have seen their tombstones, which mark the places where, side by side, they returned to dust. I cry because I cannot help it, but I thank God that their life goes on. It goes on in me and in my sister and in our children, who inherited their seed. It also goes on in the lives of those who came to know and love God as a result of their ministry.

THE WONDER OF SOIL AND SEED

The soil and the seed. The substance and the spirit. The two go together, yet each has its own cycle. The seed carries the life encoded in its nucleus, and it must be passed on to the new generation while the old generation is still alive. The flame must not die.

Soil has its own kind of continuity. Soil may rest as mud, inert and lifeless, for centuries. Then, at the touch of a seed, it becomes something new and alive. It may become part of a fruit and then be eaten and absorbed into the flesh of another living being. A few years later it returns as dust to wait in the ground for the stimulus of a new seed to wake it up so it can share in life again.

Earth and soil are so wonderful in concept and design that it is not surprising that those who live close to the earth and farm it for food sometimes develop a mystical sense that soil is life.

When, as a scientist, I begin to feel proud of what has been accomplished by men, I go out into the night and gaze up at the heavens. If it's daytime I go into the old-growth forests of our Pacific Northwest and look up at the trees. When I tire of bigness, I like to take a hand lens and lay face down exploring a single square yard of garden soil.

I encourage you to do the same. If you want to open up a new horizon of delight, buy a lens and a children's guide on soil. Get to know the worms; they are working for you, helping to grow your food. You may think of termites as enemies. Learn that for every one that eats the wood in a house, there are a thousand that work, patiently reducing fallen trees and twigs, to make new soil. Every grain of topsoil has in course of time been enriched by generations of tiny creatures, bacteria, plants, and insects. They have used the soil as a means of life and then have died, leaving the soil richer than before. Living soil is a community—billions of units of life, preparing soil for growing all the fruits we love to eat.

AGAINST ALL ODDS

My daughter Estelle and her husband and family live on the Big Island of Hawaii. They have a few acres of fruit trees and macadamia nuts. Their home is in the shadow of Kilauea, the most continuously active volcano in the world. I have looked into the boiling crater of Kilauea and have walked over recent lava flows on the coast. The ground is hot, and cracks reveal the red glow of molten rock flowing on its way to the sea. You can't get close to the actual meeting point of lava and sea, but the clouds of steam from boiling water and the red glow under the sea at the shore can be seen from a distance. There was a bay where I used to swim that is today a stretch of new land.

The island is growing. Millions of tons of molten rock are pouring out, having been forced up from deep below the ocean floor. Much of it is actively boiling as it emerges, and some is aerated as it is thrown up before it falls to become part of the new earth. Some of it will float because it is full of air, a kind of foam or sponge of rock.

All these islands have been formed that way. Estelle's house and garden stand on lava rock, and fruit trees grow in cracks. I was a skeptic when I saw the kind of "soil" in which they planned to grow their fruit and nuts, but no longer. The spongy textured rock holds water, and the roots go deep through cracks and reach to layers of soil that were built up two hundred years ago by trees and ferns that grew before the last lava flow destroyed the growth but kept the soil. They tell me that drill hole samples show that layers of soil and layers of spongy rock lie atop each other like chocolate layer cake. Those layers tell the story of how the fertile rocks hold water in their cracks and open textured sponge. They show how roots reach layers of soil protected from drying when the sun is hot.

It seems as if all of life is working together to sustain the means of life. It's not surprising that those who don't know God often see the earth itself as a living thing, perhaps a god, because they see every aspect working together for good. We know that it is God who created it and who made all things in it to harmonize for good. He left us a self-sustaining system.

Looking south from Seattle, where we live, I can see Mount Rainier floating above the clouds. I know that it must be standing on the ground, but those foundations often are shrouded in mist. The towering fourteen thousand feet of mountain challenge the climber and delight the people who commute to work, who tell each other, "Look! Rainier is out today!"

When I was young I would have found it hard to resist the challenge of a climb to the top of Rainier. Today I am content to view the floating peaks and climb around the lower slopes. I find the most exciting part of the mountain halfway up or a little higher. There, the great trees around the base give way to the smaller scrubby trees of the timberline and then to flower meadows and then a little higher to that final battleground where life struggles to maintain a foothold in little pockets of soil fighting against the winter blizzards and avalanches, against wind chill temperatures too low for life.

Against all the odds, when the snow line recedes in early summer, there they are! The exquisite alpine flowers, nodding in triumph that they have survived the chilling frost and wind. They have been buried beneath the snow but are ready to delight all who appreciate them and invite the summer bees to pollinate. The bees that winter on the lower slopes come up and fertilize the seeds that will be scattered. Most of the seeds will die because few will find one of the few islands of soil that remain.

At such altitudes, the cycle of life moves rapidly. There are not many days of sunshine and warmth for all the business of budding, flowering, fruiting, and seeding that must be completed before the first frosts of winter force the plants to withdraw from the chilling winds.

Alpine plants grow on rocks, and the plants that survive do so by clinging to fragments of soil and lichens and by forming anchors that bind the mat of roots to the rough surface of the rock.

KEEPERS OF THE FIELD

So life goes on; the cycle continues. As God's servants we have the responsibility to assist in the care of His good earth. We can have an active part in making sure that we—and others—don't interfere with God's plan for sustaining life.

I have a vivid childhood memory of someone who did just that. I was playing with a group of Indian boys in one of the rice paddies near our home in the mountains. Rice needs flooded fields for certain stages of its cultivation, and there was no level ground in the mountains. The hill tribes had developed a method of terracing their fields into the course of a stream so that each field was about a foot higher than the field below and was quite level, being bordered at its lower edge by a grass-covered dam to hold its water. Little channels were cut at intervals along the dams to allow a trickle of the stream into the field below.

Thus, where the valley was steep, the fields were narrow. They were wide where the slope was shallow. The water from the one stream watered each field in turn and kept the mud moist enough for rice cultivation. The constant wetness was attractive to frogs and small fish and also to herons, which came after the frogs. Not only herons but small boys enjoyed the mud and the frogs, and so it happened that my friends and I were having a game of who would be the first to catch three frogs. This involved a lot of plunging about in the mud in the corner of one of the fields.

Suddenly the oldest boy called out, "Tata is coming!" and we all scrambled out of the mud. *Tata* means grandfather and is used by youngsters as a term of respect for any elderly man. The particular Tata we had seen coming our way was the owner of one of the fields and was recognized as the keeper of the dams. He was the one who saw to it that nobody got more than his fair share of water when the stream was running dry. We all knew that we had not been careful with the rice seedlings, and we deserved and expected a rebuke.

Tata was very old and stooped over. He found it difficult to look straight forward. He walked slowly and with a cane, but none of us thought of running away or of avoiding his stern words. Old age really carries respect in India. He asked us what we were doing, and the biggest boy, acting as our spokesman, told him we had been catching frogs. Tata looked at the churned-up mud, then stooped over and scooped up a double handful of it. "What is this?" he asked.

"That is mud, Tata," we replied.

"And whose mud is it?"

"It is your mud, Tata, and we have broken your seedlings. We are very sorry, and we will never do it again."

But Tata had more to say. "There is enough mud in my hands to grow a whole meal of rice for one person. This same mud will grow a meal of rice every year. It has been doing it for my parents and grandparents long before I was born. It will go on growing rice for my grandchildren and their children for many generations."

"Yes, Tata."

Then the old man moved over to the nearest of the water channels across the earthen dam. He pointed to it. "What do you see there?" he asked.

"That is water," replied our spokesman.

For the first time the old man showed his anger. "I'll show you water," he growled, and limped on a few steps to the next channel, where clear water was flowing over the grass. "*That* is water," he said, and returned to the first channel. "Now tell me what you see there."

"That is mud, Tata," the boy said humbly, "It is muddy water." Then he hurried on to tell Tata what he knew would come next, for he had been exposed to this before. "This is your mud that is running down to the lower field, and it will never grow food for you again, because mud never runs uphill. Once it has gone, it is gone forever."

Tata wanted to make sure we all got the message. Leaning on his staff, he straightened his back as far as he could so he could look at each one of us. "When you see mud running in the streams of water, you know that *life* is running out of the mountains. It will never come back." He turned and began to limp away, softly repeating to himself, "It will never come back."

That was seventy years ago, but I have never forgotten the lesson I learned that day. It is a universal truth. Even in America mud never runs uphill. When we see erosion taking away our topsoil, life is flowing away from our homeland. It will never come back . . . it will never come back.

A LOSING BATTLE?

I have also learned to respect the way folk wisdom is passed from generation to generation in lands that have no schools. One of the boys I was playing with that day is probably called

Tata today, and he is patrolling the paddy fields, striking fear into the hearts of small boys and making sure that the mud of life stays in the mountains to bear fruit, rather than being washed away. We all could use some folk wisdom about how to care for the earth God has given us.

I once went along the crest of the Rocky Mountain National Park with one of the park botanists, who knew every plant by name. He pointed to a clump of tiny flowers growing from a mat of roots and soil that clung to a rocky face beside the path. The clump was perhaps eighteen inches across. "It has probably taken two hundred years for that mat of plants to grow to that size," he told us. "Some years they hardly grow at all, or even recede a bit. In a good year it may grow a quarter of an inch." He adjusted a steel post that carried a strand or two of wire fence that ran beside the path. "We always hope for early snow," he said, "because that keeps them warm, and there is a chance to grow. But it is not the blizzards that are their greatest danger; it's people."

He pointed to a family that had climbed over the fence and were sitting on rocks, eating a picnic lunch. He sighed. "They are not real bad folks, I'm sure," he said. "They just don't understand. They think these fences spoil the view or are just to stop people from picking flowers. One single step by one heavy shoe can destroy two hundred years of growth. That one step may also scrape the mat of soil from off the rock, and that place may never grow another plant. In parks like this, with thousands of visitors, we are fighting a losing battle."

What we see in miniature with alpine flowers and on Mount Rainier we see on a massive and tragic scale in Nepal and the slopes of the Himalaya Mountains. For thousands of years a sturdy simple people have lived high on those mountain slopes. Most of them live in well-watered valleys between mountain ranges. Over the centuries the Nepalese have farmed the valleys and have grown crops on the little ledges where trees have held the soil wherever the slope was shallow enough for their roots to cling.

Today the population has increased, and farming has become more aggressive. There are more cattle and goats to provide milk, and they have to go further afield to graze. More trees are cut for firewood and for homes. The wooded slopes are becoming bare. The soil is suddenly free to move, and it is moving. The rivers that once were clear are now full of mud.

Bangladesh, a country of fertile plains, has always been subject to flooding when the snows are melting on the Himalayas. The monsoon rains and melted snow fill the great rivers of the Ganges and Brahmaputra. In the past few years, and especially last year, the problem reached a new scale. Not only did the rivers overflow, but the flood was *mud*, not just water. Homes in Bangladesh were filled with mud. People drowned in mud. That mud was Nepali soil. It had grown crops for generations of mountain people, and now it was gone forever. It will never come back, and more is being lost every year, and there are more people every year depending on the crops that have less soil to grow in. Soil is eroding all over the world, and most of the problem is manmade and preventable. It is one of the great tragedies of all time, and little is being done to halt the loss. It is part of a pattern of mindless disregard for God's earth. We who claim to serve the Creator should be asking ourselves whether we are being good stewards of His great gifts.

"A FARMER WENT OUT TO SOW HIS SEED"

I feel a bit like Tata. I do not have a farm, but I try to pass on to others the lessons I have learned about soil and water and about our duty to God, who left us as stewards of His earth.

I see myself as a farmer of spiritual soil, a sower of spiritual seed. Jesus spoke about making His disciples to become fishers of men, but more often He used the picture of sowers of seed and talked about good soil and farmers.

Even as God the Creator brought life and the soil together in making the first man, so in the continuity of spiritual life, the seed and the soil have to come together to create new life and then to continue life and growth by drawing nourishment from the soil as long as life continues. To illustrate these truths Jesus told the parable of the sower and the seed. It could be titled "The Parable of the Seed and the Soil," because the only variable in the parable was the soil. The seed was the same in each example, and the sower was the same. The fruitfulness resulted from where and into what kind of soil the seed was sown.

"A farmer went out to sow his seed. As he was scattering the seed, some fell along the path; it was trampled on, and the birds of the air ate it up" (Luke 8:5).

A pathway is never a good place to plant seed. People's feet beat down the soil, smoothing out any crevices into which the seed can fall and germinate. The soil becomes hardened, and any seed that falls there will not find that openness necessary for life and growth.

In such situations the devil is quick to snatch the seed away. In a spiritual sense such people have their hearts hardened. The author of Hebrews pleads with his readers, "Today, if you hear his voice, do not harden your hearts as you did in the rebellion" (3:7–8). He was referring to the time when the Israelites were offered a chance to enter the Promised Land but turned back because they did not believe God could or would see them through. The prospect of difficulties and battles ahead made them close their minds and harden their hearts to all God had in store for them.

Living seed and sprouting wheat are not willing to share their piece of earth with booted feet. If the earth is to be a path, it may as well be paved. If it is to be soil, it must allow the seed to take over and draw nourishment and support from it. To accept the seed, soil has to become involved.

In a physical sense, there is a choice that has to be made in the use of the land. It may be used as a farm to grow food, or it may become a road and be paved for buildings and travel. The priorities of a community are revealed by the choices it makes. Today in America, prime farmland is being paved over to make way for roads and cities at a record rate. Two-and-a-half million hectares of cropland were lost to paving and building in the United States in an eight-year period in the 1970s.*

Perhaps a similar change is taking place in our mental and spiritual outlooks. Mechanical and commercial development thrives on hard surfaces. Spiritual and personal priorities need a softer soil, one that is vulnerable and open to suggestions and ideas that may require personal involvement.

Jesus looks for open hearts and minds in which to sow His seed. He looks to us, His messengers, to prepare soil by taking time to plow and hoe and soften it before we plant the seed. A good gardener does not trample over the soil he has just planted, and God's gardeners know to be gentle and loving with those who have received a seed.

USED OR USED UP?

"Some fell on rocky places, where it did not have much soil. It sprang up quickly, because the soil was shallow. But when the sun came up, the plants were scorched, and they withered because they had no root." (Matthew 13:5–6)

---

* The rate of rural land lost to development in the 1990s was about 2.2 million acres per year.

A farm is often defined by its size or extent. *For sale: five-hundred-acre farm in southern Iowa. Has been used for corn and soybeans.* I would not buy that farm until I knew a lot more about it. The words "has been used" may have many implications. Good soil, farmed by good farmers, can grow food for many generations, as Tata knew well. Iowa had deep rich topsoil when serious farming started in the last century. Today more than 50 percent of that topsoil has been lost. Much of it has been carried down the river into the Gulf of Mexico.

As topsoil becomes thinner, crops become more and more dependent on frequent rainfall and on fertilizers. Good farmers today practice the no-till method, which leaves the roots and stalks behind at harvest. They hold the soil that might be lost by plowing and enrich the soil as the roots and stalks decay, actually building the soil up year by year.

Jesus pointed out how plants grown in shallow soil are dependent on changes in the weather and cannot stand much stress. He left it to us to interpret this according to our observations. If "shallow soil" means the person who has little background knowledge of Scripture or scant experience of Christian fellowship, then we should be careful to follow the planting of the seed with fellowship and instruction in Scripture.

ROOTS IN COMPETITION

"Other seed fell among thorns, which grew up and choked the plants . . . The one who received the seed that fell among the thorns is the man who hears the word, but the worries of this life and the deceitfulness of wealth choke it, making it unfruitful." (Matthew 13:7, 22)

This parable doesn't suggest that the thorny soil was bad soil. It may have been excellent—deep and rich and moist. But it was already occupied. It had been colonized by wild thorn bushes. Their roots had penetrated deep into the soil and were consuming the nourishment that the wheat needed. Now they challenged the farmer: "Pull us out at your peril! You will have to grasp us by our thorns. It will be painful!"

In another parable Jesus said, "Ye cannot serve God and mammon" (Matthew 6:24 KJV). The farmer might say to this piece of soil, "Choose you this day what you will grow: thorns or wheat." Jesus is specific about the nature of the thorns; they take over and choke the good seed. Matthew says that wealth is a thorn; Luke adds "worries, riches and pleasures." Note that Jesus doesn't say that the good seed couldn't survive with that kind of thorn bush. What He says is that the growth didn't mature and was unfruitful.

I've already pointed out that seed is not passive in soil. The soil becomes its servant. The roots from the seed take hold of the grains of soil and use them as anchors. They extract chemical elements from the soil; they draw water from the soil to nourish the plant and to produce fruit. These demands are likely to conflict with similar demands from weeds and thorns, and a good farmer sees to it that there is no real competition.

Jesus is a demanding Lord. His coming into our hearts requires the removal of all competition. He requires that we uproot the thorns and weeds that have laid claim to the soil of our lives, so only good soil is available for the new life that is to take over and colonize our lives. Then, and only then, we shall experience the joy of fruitfulness in His service.

RICH AND FERTILE SOIL

"But the one who received the seed that fell on good soil is the man who hears the word and understands it. He produces a crop, yielding a hundred, sixty or thirty times what was sown." (Matthew 13:23)

When Jesus mentions the three kinds of soil that were not productive, He tells us why. He doesn't define the nature of the good soil except to say that it produced bountiful crops. Jesus hinted that some soil was better than others when He told the people that some seed produced a hundredfold, some sixty, and some thirty. The difference must have been in the soil.

Since the Bible does not give any clues about grading good soil, I feel free to broaden the parable to include one aspect of soil goodness that has meaning both in farming and in spiritual life. In botany the term *colonize* refers to the way a group of plants or grasses takes over a piece of land. A good example is when sand dunes have been built up by the action of tides and winds. They shift and change shape from year to year. Then seeds of some hardy type of grass may be blown into the area and begin to take root. If rain falls at the right time and roots have a chance to grow, the grasses may form a colony and begin to hold the sand together by their interlocking root systems. After a few years the plants change the nature of the sand and turn it into the beginnings of real soil. At a later stage other less hardy plants may come and take root. What was once poor soil has been transformed into good and fertile soil. Eventually the original pioneer grasses may be forgotten as the plants and trees thrive.

What has been added to the original sand to turn it into soil? The simplified answer is that it is the life and then the death of the pioneer plants. When you study a handful of good, rich soil, you will note the numerous tiny live creatures there. They are busy breaking down fragments of leaves and decaying wood, turning them into still smaller fragments that can be a source of nitrogen and phosphorus and other good things for new living plants.

My home is near the Olympic National Park and the rain forest that clothes the lower slopes of the western mountains.

We love to take our grandchildren to see the wonder of the living forest. Near the Hoh River is a row of trees in a straight line. Each one of those giant trees seems to be standing astride, with its legs apart. Each trunk is single, but only from about seven feet above ground. At that point it is supported by two huge root systems, like legs, that spread apart and curve down to reach the ground about seven feet apart, leaving a tunnel between them. If you look through the tunnel in the first tree, you can see through the other tunnels in the other trees because they are in a straight line. That clue explains it all.

A hundred years ago or more a giant tree fell in the forest. It died and lay dead and decaying for many years. Seeds, falling from other giant trees, fell into the cracks of the bark and rooted there, using the dead tree as rich soil. All the materials the old tree had collected over the years that had formed the basis of its strength and vitality were now being made available to the young seedlings growing on what we now call a "nursery log." As the young trees grew, they needed support for their great size, while the dead tree was weakened by decay. So the young trees sent out roots around the old trunk to reach the ground on either side. Those roots gradually became the whole support of the young trees, while the old tree disintegrated and finally disappeared, becoming one with the soil around it.

Our children and grandchildren have stood, quietly looking through the space where that old tree lay. We cannot see the tree itself, but we can see the way it has helped to shape and give nourishment to the new generation of giant trees, forming a "colonnade" in memory of the nursery log whose substance continues in them. I look through that space too, but with a different perspective. My active life is mostly behind me. Soon I will no longer occupy space. But I pray that my life and the principles that God has helped me to live by will continue to influence young lives. When we die we do not only leave seed, we also leave an effect on the soil in which future children grow and future spiritual seed will be nourished. That's one reason the psalmist says, "Precious in the sight of the Lord is the death of his saints" (Psalm 116:15).

Good soil is the legacy of pioneer grasses and plants now long gone. It has been said that the blood of the martyrs is the seed of the church. Perhaps it would be more accurate to say that it's the soil of the church. The seed is the living Word of God. I am thankful I grew up surrounded by a godly family who told me stories of Christian pioneers and martyrs. My heroes were those who had given their lives for Christ and the gospel. Thus, when the living seed fell into my heart, the soil was well prepared.

Now, the next question arises naturally from the last. If indeed the life of our Lord has grown in us from the seed of the Word planted there, what is the result we should expect? We read that the seed bore a lot of fruit. What is the meaning of *fruit*?

That is our next chapter.

CHAPTER 6

Fruit for All Seasons

---

*Blessed is the man who does not walk in the counsel
of the wicked or stand in the way of sinners or sit in
the seat of mockers. But his delight is in the law of the
LORD, and on his law he meditates day and night. He
is like a tree planted by streams of water, which yields
its fruit in season and whose leaf does not wither.
Whatever he does prospers.*

PSALM 1:1–3

*[Jesus said], "I am the vine; you are the branches. If
a man remains in me and I in him, he will bear much
fruit; apart from me you can do nothing."*

JOHN 15:5

Wheat farmers ask themselves several questions at harvest time. How much of the crop should be sold? How much will be needed by the family for making into bread during the year ahead? Most important, how much of the grain must be kept and set aside for planting when the soil is ready so that it may bear fruit and there may be a harvest next year too? Fruit, then, is for more than just eating. It's also for planting new seed of its own kind. It's been said that the primary biological purpose of a plant is survival of the species—that a plant or a tree is just a means of making new seed from the old. However, birds and deer—and most people—view the purpose of plants and fruit as providing food to ensure their own survival, not that of the plant. Most plant growth illustrates this. Some grasses feed the cows and sheep; others give harvests of wheat, oats, and corn. Vines bear grapes, and trees bear fruit.

So we have two different purposes for the life of plants. Do they exist primarily to make new plants, or is their purpose simply to nourish others? The answer, of course, is both, as the two objectives actually enhance each other. If animals and insects stopped eating plants and fruit and honey, many species of plants would become extinct. Bees pollinate because they like honey and pollen, not for the sake of the flower—but pollination is essential to the life of the plant.

This illustration also applies to the bearing of spiritual fruit. One primary goal of the Christian is to plant seeds so that others ultimately will come to Christ. Yet we also bear fruit so that others may benefit in the present.

BY THEIR FRUIT

I have learned much about fruit-bearing by studying some of the parables in the Bible that are based on trees. The Bible uses trees to compare the righteous with the unrighteous. Jesus said, "Every good tree bears good fruit, but a bad tree bears bad fruit . . . Every tree that does not bear good fruit is cut down and thrown into the fire. Thus, by their fruit you will recognize them" (Matthew 7:17–20). The owner of the orchard—the one who wants to eat the fruit—is the one who judges the fruit as good or bad.

Remember that the writers of these Scriptures lived in Palestine where there was plenty of sunshine and soil but not enough water. They lived on the edge of desert, and drought was an ever-present fear. To them, rivers were the symbol of a reliable supply. Over and over again Scripture uses trees to illustrate the importance of bearing spiritual fruit. The Scripture verses at the beginning of this chapter talk about "a tree planted by streams of water" and the fruit that the water enables them to bear. The tree represents us—the followers of Christ. And what is the water? The Lord himself. Spending time in Scripture—drinking in God's Word to His children—is the most effective way to receive the nourishment we need to give and bear fruit.

Trees provide an excellent picture of the spiritual life because they bear fruit, and they do so as long as they have soil and water and sun. In the same way, it is God's will that each of His children bear spiritual fruit. It is not enough that we survive; it is not enough that we grow; we must bear evidence of our growth.

RECYCLING NATURE'S WAY

Trees are a perfect example of the natural cycle living things use to obtain their nourishment from outside sources, to use these supplies for life and growth, and then to return the results of their activity to the environment in ways that help other living things grow.

Each species of tree faces different problems in different environments. The cactus and the willow have different internal structures and chemistry. One grows in the desert and has to conserve every drop of moisture, so it has thick leaves with a hard shell. The willow grows where there is plenty of water, so its soft leaves can allow free evaporation without harm. And yet, even with the wide variety of coping structures, the mechanisms of survival are the same for most trees.

Although humans have studied nature for years, modern technology continues to bring new wonders to light. Each new layer of magnification, each new insight into biochemistry gives us fresh causes for amazement for the world God has created.

Man is understandably proud of recent advancements of engineering and science. And our daily lives are made much easier by manmade products that owe their existence to science. And yet scientific achievements often result in waste, many times leaving behind waste products that are useless and sometimes harmful. Only now are we beginning to see the wisdom of recycling these end products into something useful. Yet in God's engineering, all goods and services are multipurpose from the start. The waste products of one system become the raw materials of another.

When I marvel at the wonder of trees, I am in harmony with the delight the Creator feels when He observes a forest or an orchard. Trees are aspects of His creation that have remained true to His purposes. I think God hates to see human greed spoil His creation. We get a glimpse of God's view of fruit trees in the Laws of Moses. He forbade Israel to cut down fruit trees for any warlike purpose: "When you lay siege to a city for a long time, fighting against it to capture it, do not destroy its trees by putting an ax to them, because you can eat their fruit. Do not cut them down. Are the trees of the field people, that you should besiege them?" (Deuteronomy 20:19).

IT'S THE REAL THING

When we go shopping for food, we bring home *raw* potatoes, *raw* meat, and *raw* carrots to cook into a stew. We all know what we mean by *raw*. However, a scientist would say that these foods are already carefully prepared for our use. If we were lost in a desert with really raw materials, soil and water and sun, we would starve to death. Humans can't digest the soil of which our food is made. But a tree can live on soil and water, sun and air. It knows how to use truly raw materials—while we can eat only the fruit it produces.

Jesus tells of a man who found that his fig tree had not borne fruit, so he said to the gardener, "'For three years now I've been coming to look for fruit on this fig tree and haven't found any. Cut it down! Why should it use up the soil?'

"'Sir,' the man replied, 'leave it alone for one more year, and I'll dig around it and [dung] it. If it bears fruit next year, fine! If not, then cut it down'" (Luke 13:6–9). Modern versions of the Bible say "dig around it and fertilize it," because modern man thinks in terms of commercial fertilizer, prepared in a factory for the benefit of trees. This gives us a false picture of trees being dependent on manmade food.

The King James Version of the Bible tells it like it is: the gardener was planning to "dung it." He was going to use the excrement of cattle and sheep. We use commercial fertilizer today because we don't have cows and goats in our gardens. In the Garden of Eden or in the wild, the residues of all animal droppings as well as the rotting remains of old trees and plants go back into the soil. Birds eat the fruit and drop their dung to be recycled into fresh fruit. Deer eat the leaves of the tree and say thank you by leaving their contribution to help make new leaves. When we dig around a tree and dung it we are simply reverting to what was God's original plan for feeding trees—and then people.

In our home we try to avoid throwing away anything that can be used again. We take food out of our garden. We eat the fruit, and we put back the residues as compost. It turns into flowers others can enjoy and fruit we can eat and share.

In the body of Christ we should share everything. The raw materials of spiritual life circulate from organ to organ and cell to cell. The hard experiences of one member become the fresh inspiration of another. The things that are best forgotten are taken by the blood to be discarded. The blood, like the sap of the vine, is the medium of exchange from member to member and also the guarantee of purity of the ultimate supply, extracted though it may be from a polluted environment. It is because of this remarkable system that Christians who abide in their Lord are fruitful in the hurly-burly of real life.

LIFE FROM DEATH, PURITY FROM POLLUTION

When I was a young doctor in London during World War II, I had a friend, Dr. Richard Dawson, who had been senior to me when we were students. He had joined the army and been sent to Malaysia as soon as he graduated. He returned to our medical school after the war was over to study plastic surgery. He was then working in the same unit as I. Dr. Dawson had been a lighthearted young man when he left to join the army. On his return it took a long time for him to shake off the experiences he had endured as a prisoner of war under the Japanese during the building of the infamous Burma-Siam railroad.

Dr. Dawson had been the medical officer serving thousands of prisoners of war. He had watched helplessly as hundreds died of dysentery and typhoid. He had almost no medications and no intravenous fluids to compensate for the dehydration from the fluid loss suffered by soldiers with dysentery.

Sanitation was minimal, and drinking water was often taken from swamps contaminated by the excrement of dying soldiers. Dr. Dawson could hardly bear to speak of those camps of death. The worst feature was that he himself, their medical officer, had known how to save their lives but had neither supplies nor the means to sterilize the fluids that might have saved their lives.

However, one story Dr. Dawson told was one of hope.

The prisoners were dying beside one of the steaming swamps, when suddenly Dr. Dawson remembered something about the water in a green coconut always being sterile and pure. It occurred to him that it was worth trying to use it as an intravenous infusion. It could not do harm to try on a man who was dying anyway. So Dr. Dawson sent some young soldiers climbing up coconut palms to come back with green coconuts. He cut off the fibrous ends of the fruit and drilled holes in the shell underneath. He used thin bamboo stems to form needles to push into the holes he drilled and rubber tubes to carry the fluid through needles to the dehydrated men.

Amazingly, his patients began to recover. Dr. Dawson would sit in the opening of a tent, look out over the steaming swamps that carried death, and then rest his eyes on the coconut palms that were growing out of those swamps. The trees had drawn their sap from infected water of the swamp, then filtered and purified it before putting it into the precious coconuts that were now hung in his tent. He would turn his head from the outside view of deadly swamps, then look inward to the new life flowing into his dying men. All caused by a miracle—the ability of the roots of coconut palms to turn putrefaction into purity, death into life.

There are times when Christians feel morally polluted by their environment and wonder whether they can bear good fruit under such conditions. At such times we need to remember the purity of the juice of a coconut growing in a deadly swamp. It is a reminder that our purity comes from God. When we, as a branch, abide in the vine, we will bear pure fruit.

ABIDING IN THE VINE

Jesus talks about fruit-bearing and abiding in the vine in John 15. He describes the purpose of each branch as bearing fruit; branches that don't bear fruit are cut off and thrown away. Fruit-bearing is pictured as the goal of the Christian life.

Most people interpret *fruit* as new converts to the Christian faith. I don't agree. Jesus had spoken to the disciples previously about bearing fruit. He said in Matthew 7:16 that you can tell a tree by its fruit. A good tree bears good fruit, and a corrupt tree bears bad fruit. Later, when Paul was writing to the Galatians in 5:22–23, he said that the fruit of the Spirit is love, joy, peace, patience, kindness, goodness, faithfulness, gentleness, and self-control. These all refer to qualities of life. They demonstrate what kind of life a person is living—and they are called fruit, the fruit of the Spirit.

When I interpret the parable of the vine and the branches, I put myself among the disciples on the hillside near the brook running through the Kidron Valley, where Jesus is teaching some of His last lessons before His death. He wants to tell them that even though they will soon see Him die, they may have His Spirit continue to live in them. He tries to convince the incredulous disciples that their lives will be even more fruitful if He lives in them than if He were walking beside them, as He has been doing until now. As Jesus usually did, He looked around for an object lesson.

A vineyard is close by. He points to the great bunches of grapes and explains that the branches could not bear fruit unless they remain attached to the vine, drawing their life from it, sharing its life. The fruit, the clusters of grapes that we see, are the result of abiding in the vine. They are the goal of the life of the vine and the reason the vine has branches.

This image of succulent and luscious grapes makes our mouths water. We know how good they would taste—and we want to eat them.

If grapes weren't delicious, people wouldn't eat them, and the seeds would never be spread. Think about it. When we walk along a path, eating grapes, we spit out the seeds. All along beside the path these seeds will germinate and new vines will be born.

In the biology of the Christian faith, seeds are wrapped in attractive fruit. If a vine bore only naked seeds, nobody would pick them. Everyone who wants to be a disciple of Jesus Christ is expected to bear fruit. This does not mean that we all have to be successful in bringing many people to the point of decision to become a Christian. It means our lives have to bear the taste, the fragrance, or the nourishment that makes people appreciate what we are and what we have to give. The people we work with, the members of our family or Sunday school class, should sense the pleasure and benefit of being with us. They should know that the flavor of our life comes from our abiding in Jesus Christ.

One day something may trigger the beginning of new life in someone you know who has tasted the flavor of Jesus through contact with you. We may not ever know how or when it happens. But it will be the germination of a seed that was planted because your own personal life was delicious.

I don't remember exactly when I was converted. It was not in response to a challenge from an inspiring speaker. The lives of my mother and father were dedicated to God, and their nurture of us children was an expression of God's love. I wanted to be like them and to know the spiritual resources that made their lives so fragrant. I didn't know about the seed or the new birth—but I knew their fruit, and I was attracted to it.

WHAT KIND OF FRUIT ARE YOU?

As fruit-bearers, we are expected to be food for others. Just as water quenches our thirst, we are reminded that out of us are to flow streams of living water from which others will drink.

Psalm 1 tells us to be like a tree planted by the streams of water that bears fruit every season. For whom? For others to eat and give glory to God.

Examine the quality of your life. Is your fruit attractive? Is it delicious? Are others helped by being in your presence? If not, look inside. As the heart sends blood to every member of the body, so the sap gives nourishment to others through its fruit.

CHAPTER 7

Milk: The Perfect Food

There is no finer investment for any community, than putting milk into babies.

~WINSTON CHURCHILL, RADIO BROADCAST, MARCH 1943

Like newborn babies, crave pure spiritual milk, so that by it you may grow up, in your salvation.

1 PETER 2:2

Michael Denton, a molecular biologist from Australia, has written a book called *Evolution: A Theory in Crisis*. In it he says that "the puzzle of perfection" critically challenges any theory of evolution that is based on chance mutations. New discoveries in the life sciences are opening up new levels of complexity in the workings of the living body and revealing only more and more perfection. Every organ in the body is necessary and useful, and within each organ there is an incredible inner perfection.

Today's scientific tools of investigation are much more powerful than any we had in the heyday of evolution. Now scientists can explore all the interlocking chemistry of each system. As they do they discover layers and layers of chemical reactions that act in harmony and are facilitated when they are needed and inhibited when they're not needed. This sequence of commands is written out in the DNA code that directs it all.

Such microscopic perfection dazzles the observer! It's a mathematical absurdity to think that billions of complex cells could all coordinate their precise chemistry simply by chance. Curiously, Michael Denton doesn't believe in God. He doesn't have an answer to the puzzle of perfection. But he does demonstrate that the theory of evolution is in serious crisis and that we need to find a new basis for the perfection we see around and within us.

I think of perfection when I think about God's design for providing food for newborn babies. A mother's body extracts the raw materials for the milk from a wide variety of vegetables and fruit, grains and meat that have been eaten, digested, and absorbed into the bloodstream. This milk is the perfect food for a baby; it's predigested and full of necessary nutrients. God designed a woman's body so that this process only occurs after she has given birth. It's not a continuous process—which might have been simpler to design but would have wasted a lot of milk!

Chemists and biologists have struggled for years to produce a baby formula that is as nutritious for the baby as mother's milk. Millions have been spent on research. Complex organic chemicals have been carefully selected and tried as well as methods of manufacture, all to no avail. Doctors agree—mother's milk is best. It's perfect!

RIGHT ON CUE

Every human, male and female, is born with a pair of nipples. These nipples contain all the information they need to grow into breasts and produce milk, but fewer than half of them ever do because it's not necessary. The body has many functions, such as lactation, which are possible but don't occur until they are needed and that cease when the need no longer exists. Most of these functions are controlled by special messengers, called *hormones*. Hormones are complex chemicals made in special control centers in the body. They keep each part of the body in touch with every other part. Because these hormones circulate in the bloodstream, they reach every organ and cell in the body. All the organs read each other's mail, but they respond only to their own messages.

A girl's nipples stay small and flat until puberty, when a stream of special hormones begins circulating in the blood with the message, "We are a girl! Take action." Many bones and organs then begin to make changes. The pelvis makes more room for a birth canal, the uterus begins to get ready to welcome a fertilized egg, and the nipples start making a breast.

At this stage the breast is mostly structure and fat cells. There are no milk glands—and never will be if a fertilized egg doesn't arrive in the uterus. However, when the woman becomes pregnant, a new message circulates the body, saying, "We are going to have a baby!" The breasts respond by developing a system of fine ducts that branch out all through the breast. At the ends of the finest ducts, tiny glands bud and form clusters of glands, rather like bunches of grapes. They take their time—there's no hurry—but they are ready some weeks before the baby is born, ready, but still not producing anything.

Finally, after nine months, labor begins, and hormones send a special signal that says "Go into production; milk will be needed soon."

Once the baby is born and starts feeding, how does the breast know how much milk to produce and send out? The signal for that comes from the baby! The more the baby sucks on the breast, the more milk the glands produce. So, if a woman has twins and there are two babies sucking on her breasts, she will produce great quantities of milk. She needs to eat and drink more, but everything else is automatic.

Bible writers, who knew nothing of chemistry or biology, did know the significance of milk and used it to teach us about spiritual life and growth. Peter wrote, "Like newborn babies, crave pure spiritual milk" (1 Peter 2:2). In order to understand what Peter meant, let's look at how a newborn baby desires milk.

A newborn has no prior experience in living outside her mother. She has never before eaten with her mouth. She has never heard of milk. Every sensation is new. She has to learn how to breathe air and how to interpret the signals from her eyes or her ears. But this lack of knowledge and awareness doesn't matter. When there is real need, the baby responds accordingly; the baby knows what to do.

For example, the stomach says it's empty and needs to be filled. The brain receives a signal that says, in code, that the blood sugar is low. The infant brain doesn't know what an enzyme is or why blood sugar is important, but she is programmed to respond in a certain way whenever she receives those signals. So she fills her lungs with air and then contracts her diaphragm and pushes the air out while she holds her vocal cords together, using special muscles put there for that purpose. Baby opens her mouth and cries!

Obviously the cry doesn't nourish the baby or increase the level of blood sugar; in fact, the energy to cry uses up even more sugar. But the baby's cry is the most effective signal there is. No spoken language could be more compelling.

A mother's body responds to her child's cry even before her brain has had time to think about it. Her breast has many little ducts and channels that are full of milk. These ducts have a smooth muscle around them that is relaxed until she hears the baby's cry. Then the muscle involuntarily contracts. When the baby's lips touch the nipple, even more contraction is stimulated. Sometimes the cry itself is enough to result in a little fountain of milk squirting from a duct. It's as if the breast were in as much of a hurry to supply the milk as the baby is to receive it! The mother wants to give, and the baby wants to receive.

TOO YOUNG TO FEND FOR THEMSELVES

A baby is too young to provide nourishment for herself and must depend totally on her mother for milk. This is an important reminder about the spiritual needs of newborn Christians. Even though physically and mentally they may be adults, they aren't capable of spiritually feeding themselves. They must be fed.

Today, evangelists and churches often emphasize evangelism and conversion but leave new Christians to starve because they mistakenly think new Christians can find their own food. Baby Christians need milk. Adults need it even more than children because they have so much to unlearn as well as learn. Not all churches insist on special classes for would-be members. I think this is a mistake. The churches that select their best teachers and most loving and understanding members to nurture newborn Christians are the ones that will never lack for leaders in days to come.

My grandmother understood how to nurture newborn faith. I was a child when I became a Christian. My parents, missionaries in India, left my sister and me in England with my grandmother. She and her two unmarried daughters took us into their home and were like parents to us. Our grandmother had brought up eleven children of her own and was now old and infirm. She stayed in one room, and my sister and I saw her for about an hour every evening.

I have vivid memories of Grandma. She always sat in the same big armchair with a Bible. Her eyesight was poor, so she would ask my sister or me to read the Bible to her. She would correct us if we made a mistake. We couldn't understand how she knew, without looking, that we had a word wrong until we discovered she had memorized most of the New Testament, the Psalms, and many chapters from Isaiah and other Old Testament books. When she was alone she loved to go over these passages, quoting them aloud in the night when sleep would not come. When we began to learn French at school, Grandma took out her French Bible and had us read to her. So we learned French, and Grandma's love of the Bible came through and proved to be infectious too.

Hanging on the back of Grandma's chair was a little bag full of newly minted silver coins. We did not have much money of our own, and we knew Grandma kept those coins for us. If we recited, word perfect, a verse or more of some Bible passage, Grandma would give us a sixpenny piece, which was about a quarter. A whole chapter might win us a big silver half-crown, which in today's American currency would be a couple of dollars. None of us pretended that my sister and I had memorized these Scripture verses because we loved them. We all knew we did it for money.

What Grandma knew, and we did not, was that the verses we learned would stay with us all our lives. Today, most of the Scriptures that come to mind when I need them are those I learned with my dear, cunning grandmother. Memorizing Scripture is pure milk—and it is food for growth. I strongly commend the habit, no matter the inducement.

Some of today's brightest psychologists are in advertising. They have proved that frequent repetition of simple statements soon becomes part of memory and has a profound influence on what people buy and how they behave. My dear grandmother could have told them that a century ago. She spent her life making sure her children and then her grandchildren memorized the best words, God's Word. She had us learn and repeat precepts and promises, proverbs and principles, garnished with stories of her own experience and made credible by her love and heartfelt prayers for each of us.

IMPURE MOTIVES, IMPURE MILK

Let's return to 1 Peter 2:2. The second part of the verse tells us to desire the "pure," or sincere, milk of the Word. When we describe someone as sincere we usually mean the person has pure motives. Peter, then, seems to be saying that the milk he recommends—the Bible—is pure. But this suggests that some milk could be insincere or impure. How can milk be insincere?

In an infamous baby formula scandal in Africa, a company that manufactures infant formula hired a sales force of young African women, dressed them in nurse's uniforms, and supplied them with free samples of their brand of milk formula. These saleswomen visited young mothers just after the birth of their babies and told them modern mothers don't breastfeed their babies; they use scientifically prepared milk formula instead. They gave the mothers enough free samples of formula to last several days.

Thousands of mothers accepted the samples and fed their babies with it. But when their supply of formula was gone, they discovered their natural supply of breast milk had dried up from disuse. These mothers discovered too late that they were now trapped into using the formula—which was no longer free.

While not as good as mother's milk, the formula itself wasn't bad. The problem was that in African villages there were no facilities for sterilizing baby's bottles and no reliable source for clean water to mix with the powder. The babies had no natural resistance against the infections they developed, and thousands died. The World Health Organization protested against the exploitative way the product was sold, yet the company continued the practice. It had found a new market—and big profits. Eventually, many concerned societies and churches sponsored a worldwide boycott of all the offending company's products, which affected profits enough so that the company agreed to stop its deceptive way of selling baby food.

Peter would not have called this infant formula sincere milk. The company's motive wasn't to help the babies; it was to make a profit. Unfortunately, exploitation is not limited to secular businesses. It can happen in the marketing of spiritual food, too. The Christian church has always been at its best in times of hardship, when to confess Christ invited persecution. But when the church is prosperous, individuals or organizations can also prosper financially. Leaders sometimes seek their own gain rather than the welfare of their flock. The greater the potential for financial gain, the greater the danger that the "milk" these Christians market will be insincere. We need to pray that successful preachers and Christian leaders who are successful will not become greedy for worldly gain. Paul warns Timothy to withdraw from the teachings of men "who think that godliness is a means to financial gain. But [he says] godliness with contentment is great gain" (1 Timothy 6:5–6).

A mother's milk is pure partly because she gives of herself to produce it. The baby's needs determine the composition and the quantity of the milk. That means that even if a mother is malnourished and doesn't have enough of a certain substance in her body for her own needs, her mammary glands will extract what they need for the baby, taking it from the tissues of the mother's own body. This depletes her own supply still further.

In England there used to be a saying that for every baby, the mother loses a tooth. People had observed that during lactation women lost so much calcium that their teeth developed cavities. Today, doctors and nurses see to it that a mother has a nutritious diet so that she doesn't suffer by losing her own tissues to make milk.

A mother's sacrificial giving of herself for her child is a picture of how Jesus Christ came and gave himself, the living bread, for us. He, in turn, asks that we give something of ourselves as we serve each other to help each other grow. A mother can't feed her baby something that she hasn't already eaten and digested herself, and we can't nourish others with spiritual food that we have not taken in and digested ourselves.

Others must be able to see that the Word has become part of our lives first and that it has made a difference in us.

PHYSICAL AND SPIRITUAL ADVANTAGE

I must mention one more perfection in mother's milk, something no formula can give. Most people know that milk is good nourishment and that it contains just what a baby needs for growth and strong bones. But not everyone knows this specific wonder of milk: it provides defenses against infections.

Our immune system is made up of millions of special cells that circulate through the bloodstream on the lookout for germs that might attack the body and destroy it. As soon as one of these cells meets a virus or other enemy, it studies it and organizes the making of millions of antibodies, each designed to destroy that particular kind of germ. These antibodies soon cut short or even prevent the illness.

Antibodies are built up over time. Older people, who have had years to meet many infections, usually have some ready-made antibodies left over from previous attacks, and these can go to work at once, without waiting for the earlier stage of design. But babies haven't had time to meet and overcome any infections, so they easily catch any disease going around and may become ill and even die before they have time to make their own antibodies.

This is where mother's milk comes in. Some of the mother's own antibodies are transferred to the baby through the milk. So the baby can fight her first battles against infection using her mother's antibodies. No manufactured milk formula in the world can do this! Mother's milk is unique.

Like the mother who shares her defenses against infections with her baby, mature Christians can help younger Christians develop spiritual antibodies. Too often more mature believers are shy to confess their problems and weaknesses. This gives the impression that the older Christians live on a different plane of holiness and have never struggled. We forget that when we expose our weaknesses we are able to share how God has helped us handle them.

In Hebrews 2:18 the apostle tells us that because Jesus experienced suffering and temptation, He is able to comfort those who are tempted. The same is true for us. The person who has met temptation and overcome it in the power of the Spirit is better able to help young Christians who are meeting the same kind of temptation themselves. Mature Christians who nurture a new believer should be able to give insights learned from past battles and past victories to help the young Christian grow and ward off temptation. They can also be helpful in helping newborn Christians to be spiritually discerning.

LEARNING TO DISCRIMINATE

Babies are not born with the ability to discriminate—and milk guarantees that they don't need to. Milk is predigested food and is safe for the baby. Paul says, in Hebrews 5:14, that solid food is for those who have learned by experience to discriminate between what's good and what's evil.

Human brains are complex; they take time to develop. When a baby is born only the most basic parts of the brain are ready. Babies know how to regulate breathing, how to suck and swallow, and how and when to cry. That's about it. Their time is spent discovering new things, and because the lips and tongue are sensitive, everything within reach goes into the mouth.

When babies start to crawl, they find still more things to put into their mouths. They are curious about everything. They see it, touch it, and put it in their mouths. If it tastes interesting, they may swallow it. If it tastes nasty, they spit it out. Mothers spend a lot of time taking things out of babies' mouths, using their words and tone of voice to teach their children about what they shouldn't eat.

A child has to learn by experience what is good and what is bad. Milk is a guaranteed supply of good food that can last until the child is ready to choose for him or herself.

All babies eventually need to be weaned. If they don't make the transition from milk to solid food, their growth and maturity will be hindered.

Most mothers begin the weaning process during the first year. They start to introduce solids into the diet at five or six months and then gradually develop more variety. In India and Africa mothers may go on nursing for two or more years because there are not many fine pureed foods available. At this age the child usually begins to assert his individual preferences. Two-year-olds are fully mobile, inquisitive, and have developed a strong self-will but still no discrimination. They are into everything, and if not watched carefully, could easily hurt themselves. Households with two-year-olds echo with the sound of "no!"

This age is an ideal time for parents to lay the foundations for spiritual growth. The quality of love and care that surrounds the toddler is the food for building the spiritual framework in which future character and Christian faith will grow.

Toddlers absorb lasting impressions from every experience. It's a time when the child is teachable and open to developing such character qualities as truthfulness (Do the parents really mean what they say?), justice, anger, forgiveness, love, ownership of property, punishment, and fairness. Everything learned is tested again and again to see if it is real. Most of these significant principles are embraced unconsciously during those early home years.

Parents who want to know what is influencing their children have a great challenge ahead of them. With the invention of television came the potential problem of strangers infiltrating our home and offering entertainment and pretty things to our children without our knowledge. Television can influence a child's choice of words and acceptance of ideas, and the parent has no idea where the child has learned them.

What are even more dangerous are the subtle assumptions behind most television programs. Violence is depicted as an appropriate way to settle disputes. "Falling in love" is applauded as a good reason for a married person to leave a spouse and link up with someone new. Lying is often pictured as a clever and often funny way to get out of difficult situations.

Television's potentially negative influence often directly competes with the spiritual food parents give their children in their desire to rear children with character and who love God. Allowing young children to watch TV unsupervised is like letting them loose in a house where poisons are left on low shelves in bottles marked "honey." They don't know what they're dealing with.

When our first baby was not yet two years old, we found him on the floor with an open bottle in his hand that contained Phenobarbital tablets. He smiled as he held it up and said "sweeties!" They belonged to the previous owner of the room, who had left them in a low drawer. No one knew how much young Christopher had eaten, so we rushed him to the hospital to have his stomach pumped.

He didn't know any better. He was just too young to discriminate. The tablets were good for the person who needed them but might have been deadly for the exploring child.

It takes longer to develop discrimination than many of us realize, and those who care for young children need to be as careful about what the mind absorbs as every mother is about the physical food her baby gets.

STEPS TOWARD MATURITY

Babies are incapable of making decisions and taking any responsibility for their well-being and growth. That is the job of the parents. But as they get older, that begins to change. As they take a greater variety of solid food, so they begin to take some responsibility for their own nourishment. Some independence must be encouraged. A wise mother entices her child to taste solid foods and take some initiative.

This is also an important stage of spiritual growth. We have to take God at His word. We must move into situations where we have to depend on the power of the Holy Spirit, as in when we first make our faith known to secular friends. When there is nobody to prompt us as to what to say, it tests the reality of our spiritual life.

When the children of Israel were being formed into a new nation in the wilderness, God fed them with manna, a complete food they did not have to work for. It was like mother's milk. The story of what happened next is a good lesson for us as we hesitate to take responsibility in our own Christian lives.

CHAPTER 8

No More Free Lunch

Jesus answered, "I tell you the truth, you are look-
ing for me, not because you saw miraculous signs but
because you ate the loaves and had your fill."

JOHN 6:26

"My food," said Jesus, "is to do the will of him who
sent me and to finish his work."

JOHN 4:34

It was the early 1950s in India. We had finally discovered how to successfully reconstruct the hands and feet of people who had been deformed by leprosy.

Margaret and I had assumed that once the disease was cured and the hand deformity was corrected, our patients would be able to go back to their own villages and find work. We were wrong. The village people did not quite believe that leprosy could be cured. They could see that the hands were improved, but they saw that the patients had to take special care not to injure themselves because they did not have a normal sense of pain.

Some of our first patients who had gone home with reconstructed hands came back months later, still unemployed. Hungry and discouraged, they said they had tried to get work and had showed their good hands. But they were rejected because they still bore the marks of leprosy on their faces. Nobody wanted to employ a leprosy patient, even if the doctors said he was healed. I felt their discouragement; they were just like my own children. I made the decision that we would not send patients home to their villages until they had some means of livelihood, some trade that would make it possible for them to support themselves. I would somehow raise funds to build a village just for these patients. We put up huts of sun-dried mud bricks and thatch. We built sheds with work benches where we could teach carpentry. We bought sewing machines so tailoring could be taught. We had therapists to train their hands and cooks to prepare meals and teach them how to cook without harming their insensitive hands. We even had land and an agriculture program for those who wanted to learn how to farm.

All of this was planned with the idea that these former patients could become independent. Even if nobody would employ them, they could work for themselves. Now, when young men were finished with their surgery, we admitted them in to our new rehabilitation village. We called it Nava Jeeva Nilayam (the Place of New Life). They loved it, and I loved it too. It became the focus of my life. We developed little industries. We made wooden toys and plastic devices to sell in a little store in the same village.

People crowded in to see what leprosy patients could do and went away with purchases. The news spread that people who had been beggars with leprosy could now work and produce beautiful articles for sale. What an exciting time for all of us!

But, as the numbers of patients increased, the time came to send the first patients away to make room for more. We thought a few weeks or months of training would be enough to give them confidence for a new life and for independence. In many cases it was, but we found that life in Nava Jeeva Nilayam had become just too attractive.

Back in their own villages, our rehabilitated patients thought back wistfully to the free food, the good tools, and snug sleeping quarters. It made it difficult for them to accept their independent status and uncertain employment and the leaky sheds where many of them had to sleep.

Some asked for attention to a wound, and others asked for more instruction in a trade. Some offered to become instructors, while others wanted help in selling some of the articles they had made. They told us their own village had no market for the unfamiliar Western-style things we had been able to sell easily in the city. Everybody had different reasons, but they all added up to a wish to come back into the sheltered environment we had created for them.

We asked the advice of others who were older and more experienced. We asked those who had worked to rehabilitate the blind or the lame or just the very poor. They all told us the same story and said they were sure it would apply to leprosy patients as well. They told us that we had created a nest that was too comfortable and that we would have to be a little cruel to be really kind. They pointed to the biblical lesson of the eagle that has to stir up its nest (Deuteronomy 32:11) to drive out the young eagles that become addicted to being fed by their parents. They have to learn to fly on their own, even though the parent bird spreads its wings to catch them in case they fall.

Nava Jeeva Nilayam had become like an eagle's nest. It was too easy, like growing up on a mother's breast. Rehabilitation would be surer and more successful if nobody stayed in the center for more than a short, controlled period of time.

Today the center is still there, but it serves more as a memorial to those exciting days. Now, leprosy patients return to their villages after surgery and a brief training. We prefer to provide help right in the village where they live. It's more difficult for our helpers and instructors who now have to travel to many villages, but rehabilitation is more successful if we don't give them an opportunity to become dependent.

ADDICTED TO THE EASY LIFE

We all have a lazy streak in our character, and if food is free and plentiful, we are in danger of becoming addicted to the easy life. Just look at the children of Israel.

As slaves in Egypt, the Israelites were forced to do heavy labor. In exchange, they were fed. In some common eating place, food was prepared for them and made available in what they later referred to as *fleshpots*.

But when Moses led the Israelites into the wilderness, they lost their regular, dependable supply of food. The newly formed nation had no experience or skill in finding food in the wilderness, and so they whined and cried for help. In response God fed them in a miraculous way until they reached the Promised Land.

Every morning the Israelites found food scattered on the ground around the camp. They called it *manna*, which means "What is it?" All they had to do was to collect it and eat it. They didn't need any other foods as it contained all the calories, protein, carbohydrates, fat, vitamins, and minerals that they needed for their nourishment. They sometimes grumbled about the lack of variety but were happy that it involved no work.

In a sense manna was just like mother's milk. God, the great provider, was giving the Israelites a balanced diet, a complete food. This was good, except that they became dependent on it and began grumbling about other things they felt they needed. I marvel at the patience of Moses, but even he had his limits. In Numbers 11:12–14, we read of his utter disgust when he was faced with the demands of the Israelites for fresh meat. Moses turns to God and asks why he has been burdened with these people. He cries, "Did I conceive all these people? Did I give them birth? Why do you tell me to carry them in my arms, as a nurse carries an infant ... The burden is too heavy for me." Moses recognized how manna had become like mother's milk (or father's milk, as he saw it!).

God agreed that the situation was too much for Moses and arranged help. He also demonstrated to the people that they were not discriminating about what they ate. When large flocks of quail appeared miraculously over their camp, the people gorged on meat and became sick. As a nation, they still were not ready for weaning.

I suspect that the children of Israel's dependence on manna contributed to their unwillingness to respond to the challenge of the Promised Land. The Bible is not explicit about this, but I read the implication clearly in the story of their miserable retreat.

The children of Israel must have been excited to have reached the border of the land that was to become their own homeland. Twelve spies were sent out, and they came back carrying samples of the fruit of the land. It was indeed a land flowing with milk and honey. But the spies told them there were difficulties: giants, walled cities, and probable battles.

Joshua and Caleb encouraged them to go ahead and trust that the Lord would help them win the land. As they listened to the report of the spies, I suspect that most of the crowd may have been muttering, "Why should we expose ourselves to danger and to fighting? We have a pretty good life here in the wilderness. We have a good balanced diet. We don't need to till the soil or plant crops or harvest them. We don't need to fight. We have a choice about this. We can choose toil and sweat and danger over there, or we can have good food without working for it right here."

God was angry. He was angry they were unwilling to do anything for themselves, even though they were assured of God's help. They wanted to be nursed like babies and fed on miracles.

Because they had refused the challenge God offered them, the people of Israel were condemned to forty more years of manna and wandering, forty more years with no purpose except to go on living until they died in the wilderness.

Forty years passed, and a new generation of Israelites grew up. Again they reached the borders of the Promised Land. Now Joshua and Caleb, the spies who had wanted the people to go forward the first time, were the leaders. Joshua crossed the river Jordan, and the people saw the river open up to the footsteps of the priests and the ark. The miracle excited them. There was a good chance they would go ahead and take the land.

But God was taking no chances this time. Israel had proved how fickle she could be. "The Israelites celebrated the Passover. The day after the Passover . . . they ate some of the produce of the land . . . The manna stopped the day after they ate this food from the land; *there was no longer any manna for the Israelites*, but that year they ate of the produce of Canaan" (Joshua 5:10–12, italics added).

The Israelites now had to advance and take risks or they would starve. God knew how difficult it had been for the earlier generation to make a hard choice. Why work if you can receive welfare? So God made the hard choice for them: no more free food. It was time for them to grow up and fend for themselves.

STRETCHING BEYOND YOUR COMFORT ZONE

Jesus recognized the same attitude in the Jews after He had fed the five thousand. The people crowded after him across the lake, looking for more free food. It's a universal problem:

People don't want to be challenged and stretched beyond their comfort zones.

It happened in Israel, it happens in India, it happens in the United States, and it even happens in our churches. People who have been Christians for years delight in coming to church week by week. They listen to the greatest Bible teachers but never accept the challenge to test their faith in real life. They never step outside of their safe, Christian environment where there is no conflict. They enjoy teaching about their duty to the poor and needy as they sit in their padded pews and then go home to Sunday supper. They are happy to learn how to witness for Jesus Christ, but only in a place where everybody is a believer.

If you and I are enjoying a comfortable church with fine preaching but with no responsibility and no stimulus to go out and put our faith to the test, we won't grow. God requires that each of us accept the challenge to search His Word for ourselves and seek His will for work He wants us to do.

You and I need to cross the river Jordan; we need to overcome our fear and enter the Promised Land. Joshua challenged the people to possess a land where there was to be fighting; there was to be plowing and hoeing and harvesting. They would face overwhelming odds, but the Lord was to be with them. When Jesus challenged the disciples to go into the world and preach, He was also promising His presence to go with them and provision for their need.

CHAPTER 9

Unwashed Hands

Cleanliness of body was esteemed to proceed from a due reverence to God.

~ Francis Bacon

Nothing outside a man can make him "unclean" by going into him. Rather, it is what comes out of a man that makes him "unclean."

Mark 7:15

I was in India during Lent a few years ago and was asked to preach at an Episcopal church that had become part of the Church of South India. I knew they followed the Christian calendar, so I asked for the prescribed subject and readings for the day. I was surprised when the presbyter apologized that the subject was piety. It was as if he thought it was a difficult, or perhaps an old-fashioned, subject, and I was surprised when I found that I was uncomfortable with it as well. I had never preached on that subject before, and perhaps it evoked an image of otherworldliness that did not fit with the kind of active involvement that I like to encourage in a church. However, I agreed and asked for the prescribed Bible readings. There was a reading from Jeremiah and another from James. Everything seemed to fit until I came to the reading in Mark.

Jesus was being criticized for eating without washing His hands and letting His disciples do the same. The passage included the defense that Jesus gave for His action and His attitude. I couldn't see the connection between washing and piety. If there was a connection, it would seem that a pious person would give his hands an extra wash, not be making excuses for not washing.

I sensed God had a message to give and had chosen me to speak it. I knew I had the Holy Spirit to give me insight about what to say, so I closed my eyes and allowed pictures to drift through my mind. I focused on the word *piety*, and I saw a stained glass window in an old church in England. There was a picture of a saint dressed in flowing white robes. She was looking forward, and her hands were together, palm to palm. As a hand surgeon, I always notice the hands of anybody I meet, so I focused on hers. They were slender, white, and *clean*. I found it odd that they were held together, palm to palm, as if she didn't want to touch anything. I wondered why.

Then I remembered that I sometimes stand, looking around, with my hands held together when I'm about to operate. I follow a rigid routine. It begins with washing my hands with a sterilized scrubbing brush, and then I scrub each finger tip, under each nail, and between each finger. Next I scrub each knuckle, first with the finger straight, then fully flexed to open up the cracks of the folded skin on the back of the knuckle. (A germ might hide in a crease of the skin.) I scrub up to my elbows and then do it all again in case I missed a bit the first time. Finally, I dip my hands in alcohol and lift them to allow any fluid to drain off from my elbows. (It would be foolish to allow water or alcohol to drain off the other way, from my unclean upper arms down to my well-scrubbed finger tips.)

I dry my hands on a sterile towel and am helped into a sterile gown and sterile rubber gloves. I wear a mask to prevent my breath from carrying infection into a wound. Now I'm ready.

Then the anesthesiologist at the head of the table says, "Just a minute, doctor! I don't think the patient is quite ready. I need to give a little more of this or that so the muscles will be relaxed. I'll tell you when we are ready." So I wait.

Normally, if I had to wait, I would *do* something. I'd make some notes, blow my nose, scratch my neck, polish my glasses. But not now. I have to stay pure; not just clean but sterile; not one germ must be on my hand or glove. *That* is when I put my hands together and hold them there. If I leave them hanging, I might forget and touch something. And I would have to start all over again, taking off my gown and gloves and scrub ten more minutes before putting on a new gown and gloves.

Why all this fuss? Because I'm about to go *inside* a person. I am about to make an incision, cutting through the skin that defines and separates the world outside from the absolute purity and sterility of a person's inside world. If my patient develops an infection after the operation, everyone will know that I was the one who let it in. I carried an enemy germ in through the natural defenses. The invasion of that purity and sterility would have been my fault. So I put my hands together. I am preoccupied with purity.

My meditation on piety continued.

As I tried to imagine Jesus' hands at the time the Pharisees complained that He and the disciples had not washed before they ate their food, I realized that the pious image in the stained glass window looked more like a Pharisee than like Jesus. The Pharisees were preoccupied with ceremonial purity. They were the ones who walked carefully down the street lest they touch anything or anybody who might contaminate them. Perhaps they held palms together as they walked, lest they touch a sinner.

Now I understood Jesus' reply to their accusation. It was as if He said, "If I were going to cut through the skin and operate on a person, I would scrub my hands and put on sterile gloves, because I'd be going *inside*. As it is, we're just going to eat food. It can go through the body and not cause any real contamination. We should be concerned about the evil thoughts that are already inside. They come out as evil words. They reveal the pollution inside."

Of course I knew that the Pharisees were speaking of ceremonial washing. But the pictures drifting through my mind that day showed a group of men who followed Jesus day after day, week after week, walking from village to village and having no home or house to return to at night. They had no washing machine or dryer and sometimes not even a basin, let alone a bath. If they passed by a well, somebody might offer to draw water for a drink and a wash, out in the open. I doubt that there was any soap by the well.

I made some notes and wrote down this insight: "Perhaps the hands of Jesus really were dirty; at least by the standards of the people who came from nice homes." Then my mind picked up on some half-forgotten memories of my own hands and fingernails in the days when I had been a manual worker as an apprentice plumber in the building trade in England. I lodged in the home of a stonemason and adopted his ways and manners. On weekends I went home and spent Sunday in our church in St. John's Wood, an upper-class suburb of London.

During that time I lived two lives. Each weekend I would creep back into my home and have a hot bath, settling down for a long and painful session with abrasive soap and a nail brush. I would try to trim my broken fingernails and get under the cuticle with more soap. In those days plumbers worked with lead. (That's why they are called plumbers, from the Latin for *lead*.) We used lead pipes and lead paint and red lead oxide for sealing pipe junctions. Lead stains the skin and doesn't wash off easily. I needed pumice stone to rub off the outer layers of my skin before it began to look clean.

Finally I would put on my Sunday clothes and go to church. When I entered my church I often hid my hands, the evidence of my other world. If I had gone to a church dinner and eaten as I usually ate in the home of my stonemason host, my friends would probably frown, saying, "Who is this that eats with unwashed hands?" England in those days was very class conscious.

Jesus and His followers were definitely lower class in Judea. The scribes and Pharisees were upper class and made sure their clean robes were not defiled by contact with people who might pollute them. However, they came to listen to Jesus, as they had listened to John the Baptist, and must have recognized that when it came to true morality and godliness, Jesus held the high ground. When Jesus said the Pharisees were like "whitewashed tombs," He implied that washing hands does not remove defilement any more than whitewashing tombs removes decay from inside the tomb. I knew that Jesus' hands must often have been dirty and that He would not hide them just because Pharisees were around.

My sermon on piety that Sunday focused on Mark 7:18–23 and the words *outside* and *inside* and then on James 1:27: "Religion that God our Father accepts as pure and faultless is this: to look after orphans and widows in their distress and to keep oneself from being polluted by the world." I shortened that verse to a brief three-word motto for piety: "compassion without contamination."

True religion demands that the Christian go out into an impure world, bringing the love of Jesus to the neediest. Jesus wasn't afraid of contact with sinners because His heart and mind couldn't be contaminated.

Jesus' example makes it clear that getting ourselves involved in a dirty world need not mean that we are going to become contaminated ourselves. Our hands may indeed be dirty, but we can keep the contamination outside while letting compassion flow from inside.

I believe we can confidently seek the help of the Holy Spirit when we meet and work with people whom we feel we can love and help in His name, however bad those individuals may be. In the one-on-one relationships we may be led into, God is committed to use and enhance our love and our effort and to protect our own integrity in doing so. We are actually strengthened by such activity, as though we had had a spiritual meal.

How is it that we are protected from the impurities of those outside of faith in Christ? What is the nature of the barrier that protects us as we move in a sinful world? Is it always reliable? I think some illustrations from biology might give us a picture of how we remain protected from harmful influences.

INSIDE IS OUTSIDE

I want to take you for a quick walk past various types of life, to see how, in every case, there is always an *outside* and an *inside* and that they are kept clearly defined.

Let's begin with amoebae, the single-celled creatures that inhabit the ponds and oceans. An amoeba has a delicate membrane that encloses the cell. This membrane keeps everything out that should be kept out and lets everything in that is needed inside, including food. What's inside that membrane is amoeba, and what's outside is the rest of the world.

At mealtime the amoeba may bump into a speck of stuff and decide that it might be good for food. It has no stomach, so it makes one by changing its shape. It makes a little hollow, like a dimple, on its surface where the food is. Then the edges of the hollow rise up and reach over the speck of food and enclose it completely, fusing over the top. The speck of food is now in a little balloon made of the same membrane that is the skin of the rest of the amoeba. So now the cell, which looks like a balloon, has a little balloon inside it. Inside the little balloon is a speck of food being analyzed and digested by chemicals that the big balloon pours into the little balloon. The little balloon is called a vacuole.

The good food is absorbed into the main body of the amoeba and the little balloon moves back to the surface of the main membrane. It opens to the outside world and changes from functioning as a stomach to functioning as a rectum, ejecting the unwanted residue. Finally, the sides of the little balloon flatten out and return to being just part of the outside membrane covering the amoeba.

I must emphasize that even when the membrane forms a smaller balloon to serve as a stomach, it still keeps the outside surface outside and the inside, inside. Try to imagine poking your finger into an inflated balloon. You push some balloon fabric inward, and your finger looks and feels as if it were inside the balloon. But it's not, because your finger is touching the outside of the balloon. If your finger had been dipped in perfume, the inside of the balloon would not smell it unless it seeped through the fabric of the balloon.

This is how it is when an amoeba makes a small balloon around a speck of food. So whether the small balloon is serving as a stomach or intestine for absorption or as a rectum for elimination, it still separates the outside from the inside; everything inside the small balloon is outside the amoeba.

There is a strange little animal that takes its food in through its foot. A gastropod, which means "stomach-foot," is an animal that glides along, like a snail, on its one foot. This foot has some sort of taste sensor, so when a gastropod stands on something edible, it knows it.

It opens up its stomach, which is inside its foot, and turns it inside out. If you pick up the gastropod at that point and look at the sole of the foot, you see what looks like a whole bunch of rootlets, or projections, that we call villi. These little root-like buds pour out digestive juices and dissolve the stuff the gastropod is standing on. Then the dissolved food is sucked into the inside of the animal. At the end of the meal the gastropod pulls its stomach in again and goes on walking on its foot.

Whether the stomach is facing out as a projecting root or facing in as a cavity, the real outside surface is always outside, and the food has to be analyzed as it goes inward through the discriminating membrane of the stomach.

A gastropod has to stand still while it is eating and remain standing while the food is digested and absorbed. When God made men and women, He gave us a mouth, stomach, intestines, and rectum. I can walk and run and jump and climb without worrying about whether I should be digesting what I am walking on. When I do eat, I put my food into a continuous passage that does, in sequence, what an amoeba has to do with one piece of its skin, and I don't even have to think about what the different parts of my alimentary canal are doing. They all know what to do.

The human alimentary canal does, in a more efficient way, what all stomachs do. The result is that food is digested while it is still technically outside the body. Then nutrients are absorbed through a discriminating membrane into the inside of the body. Finally, the residue is eliminated and never absorbed into the body.

Thus, in all living creatures, there is a sharp distinction between outside and inside, and every creature has a discriminating barrier through which anything that is to be absorbed has to pass.

THE BODY'S IMMIGRATION DEPARTMENT

Different parts of the body are exposed to different kinds of stress or danger, and each of the coverings of our bodies is designed to protect us from exactly the dangers that threaten that particular area of the body.

The anatomical word for the outer layers of skin is *epithelium*, and we speak of different kinds of epithelium for the different kinds of protection that the body needs. The epithelium on the hands and feet is thick and many-layered so that it can protect the body from hard, rough objects that might otherwise break the skin and infect the body. It also protects from germs.

The epithelium of the eye is transparent so that we can see through it. It is delicate, so it needs to be covered in times of danger by folds of tougher skin on the eyelids. The mouth and throat are covered on the inside by a slippery skin kept moist by saliva. All the way down there are special kinds of epithelium that allow digestive juices to flow out and that accept digested food in fluid solution to enter the body through tiny well-guarded openings. The lining is clearly marked "outside" on one side and "inside" on the other.

The lining in the human stomach and intestines looks like a forest of tiny sprouting rootlets. The little root buds are called *villi*, and they grow out from the lining of the intestines and lie in the fluid soup that is made up of all that we have eaten and chewed up and swallowed. In the stomach and intestines this food has been digested, and now every little element just lines up to be inspected by the immigration department of the body at the surface of the nearest of the villi.

At rest, those little villi are rather pale, but when a load of food is on its way down, the villi begin to blush, due to a sudden increase of blood supply. Food is on its way. Blood that has been busy helping the brain to think or muscles to work, finds that those arteries are being narrowed, while arteries and veins in the intestines are opening up. The blood goes where there is work to do.

Heavy work and creative thought may have to be put on hold while blood is diverted to digestion. My own brain is quick to tell me that I should not try to prepare lectures or write books just after lunch. It refuses to work when it has too little blood. It easily convinces me that I might as well lie down and wait until my intestines are less busy and are willing to release more blood for the brain.

After lunch there has to be plenty of blood ready to make digestive juices to pour into the intestines and also to receive new molecules of food and water into the body. These are sucked in through the microscopic pores of the villi, where they have been inspected and approved. The blood carries the newly admitted material to the liver, the chemical factory of the body, where it will be sorted out and built up into the kind of chemicals that the body needs. The liver is also a place where harmful chemicals can be destroyed. If something toxic has escaped the screening at the immigration department, the liver breaks it down into simple harmless units such as urea that can be expelled by the kidneys.

Further down the intestines, the fluid soup has gradually given up most of the nourishing food that it carried and is mostly just watery juices and indigestible material. This is made up of fibers and some little lumps that have never been chewed and are too tough for the chemicals to dissolve. There may also be some harmful materials that were turned away by the villi higher up.

Here a whole army of friendly bacteria get to work on things that are indigestible to humans. They break them down into simpler chemicals, some of which can then be absorbed by the villi in that segment of the bowel wall. The germs in our large bowel eat the stuff that our intestines could not absorb, turning some of it into food.

FRIENDLY, BUT NEVER INTIMATE

Though friendly, these germs cannot and must not get inside the body. They stay on the outside, though they work for us and we use their products. It they did enter we would have independent living cells inside our bodies. They would not be subject to the discipline of the body and the head. This would be an infection. Our defensive cells would recognize them as foreign and would attack and destroy them. If they failed, our whole body might be taken over by hostile cells, and we might die. As a surgeon I have to be careful when I operate on intestines that I do not allow any of the contents of the lower bowel to escape into the inside of the body.

What a wonderful membrane we have in our gut! It allows us to do business with all sorts of creatures and yet always to know that we associate with them for business purposes only. We must never allow them to jeopardize our loyalty to our head. They have their own primary loyalty, which is to themselves. We can be friendly but never intimate.

This is, in a limited way, a picture of our relationships with the world around us. The Lord calls us to associate with the ungodly and sinners, as Jesus did. We may do business with them, and we may count them among our friends. Yet we must never let down our guard. We are a committed people, members of Christ's body, and our loyalty to our body must never be compromised by inviting inside one who does not share that loyalty.

These membranes that divide inside from outside function only while there is life. When death comes, even though the membranes look the same and the chemicals that they are made of have not changed, they stop being effective immediately. It takes *life* to make them work.

When I have operated on human intestines, I marvel that their thin membranes are able to protect the purity of the body from the contamination and bacteria that are in the colon, only a millimeter away. By contrast, when I have to perform an autopsy on someone recently dead, I see an ugly staining of what had been pure and can detect infection where during life it was sterile. In death, the contents of the bowel are no longer kept outside. The membranes are still intact, but now inside is open to outside, and corruption sweeps through the gates that now swing idly open.

For all the advances of science, we still cannot define life. We do not understand its nature or how it sustains the integrity of a membrane that loses its effectiveness just moments after death. We know the chemistry of each of the elements of the living cell, but if we assemble them together it still does not make life. We can define life only by what we see it doing.

It is somewhat the same with spiritual life. One of the signs of the reality of the life of the Spirit within us is that it keeps our membranes functioning effectively. If we are alive in the Spirit and the Spirit lives in us, it is possible to go out into the impure world and mix with sinners, ministering to those who need the love of Jesus Christ, and yet we ourselves do not become polluted. The discrimination that protects us is not the structure of the Ten Commandments or the strength of our moral code. It is the life of the Spirit that keeps us sensitive, minute by minute, to the human needs outside and to our personal need for holiness within. When we see this beginning to happen, we may recognize it as a sign of life, the beginning of genuine piety.

Others may know theology and memorize the Bible. Like the Pharisees, they may have great concern for keeping spiritual laws and give tithes of all they possess. They may pray and sing praises to God. They may be identified as Christians, and yet Jesus may say, "I never knew you. You do not share my *life*."

LIFE IN FELLOWSHIP

Although every living cell has a skin of some sort, a membrane that limits and defines it, there is a big difference between living cells that are part of a larger life, like cells of a human body, and those that live exposed to the environment as single cells, like amoebae. The latter have always to be on guard against real enemies and deadly heat or cold. Their defenses need to be strong and always alert.

Of the trillions of cells in a human body, most are surrounded on all sides by friendly cells that share the same loyalty to the head and that live together in harmony. They never experience extremes of heat or cold, never become dried out or come into contact with poisons. They can afford to let down their guard, and they benefit by the exchange of fluids and nourishment with other cells around them, without a sense of competition.

We should not press this metaphor beyond its natural limits. But I think it is fair to point out the benefits of Christian community and of the living body of the family, both in the matter of defense and in the sharing of good food. Single cells are always preoccupied with defense. They are dominated by the sense of competition. Eat or be eaten. Be thick-skinned or perish.

But in a body of cells, the life is shared; both the protection of that life and the successful growth are undertaken as a corporate task. The individual cells are not on their own. Within the body of Christ, within each local body of believers and within each family, we can enjoy the special privileges of being part of an organic structure. Even when our individual role involves standing up in defense of the life of the body as a pioneer or a martyr, we go forth as a member of a life-giving whole.

Within the community of faith, we should take advantage of opportunities for lowering our guard. We should seek out the close friendship of likeminded members and get to know each other as only those can who are willing to come out from behind their defensive shells and become vulnerable.

In marriage, two people become one flesh, which means that there are no barriers, and each becomes vulnerable to the other. In that sweet intimacy there can be true sharing. An atmosphere is created that promotes trust and friendship as the family widens with the arrival of children. ·

The words "they shall be one flesh" are descriptive of the merging of two lives, almost to the extent that they share the same skin. Such oneness is the basis of future happiness for themselves and for the children whose security is bound up also in that same identity of shared life.

Intimacy and vulnerability go together. A husband and a wife each know the other so well that they are in a position to cause more intense pain than anybody else can cause. It is a refined cruelty because it happens from within shared confidences and lowered barriers. The result inevitably is a hardening of the cell membranes and the development of defenses that isolate one from the other.

Before this book is published, my wife Margaret and I will, God willing, be celebrating fifty-five years of oneness and will be doing it with the continuing oneness of each of our children. Some of our twelve grandchildren are too young to know the factors that are even now shaping their lives. Not least of those factors is the security of a close family, of being surrounded by an intact external "epithelium" that allows them to be open and receptive to the love within that family bond.

CHAPTER 10

A Banquet of Variety

A surfeit of the sweetest things,
The deepest loathings to the stomach brings.

~ WILLIAM SHAKESPEARE,
MIDSUMMER NIGHT'S DREAM

How sweet are your words to my taste,
sweeter than honey to my mouth!

PSALM 119:103

Dr. Victor Rambo, the chief of ophthalmology at our Christian Medical College in Vellore, India, had a favorite object lesson he used when he spoke in our chapel services. He would fill a glass tumbler to the brim with water, and at just the right moment in his address, he would pick it up and take a sip. Someone close by on the platform had been primed to nudge him at that moment, and the water would spill over onto his shirt. He would laugh and say to the clumsy fellow, "Don't apologize. It doesn't matter—there was only water in the glass." Then he turned to us and commented that times of stress can bring out of us only what is already inside. The only way to avoid spilling out dirty stuff is to make sure there is no dirty stuff inside.

I remember vividly my own struggle with words and grammar when I began to work on construction sites in the building trade. I was working with men who had only the simplest education, and their talk was pure Cockney slang, the street language of London from ages past. My natural speech was pedantic and correct. It could be called Oxford English. But I wanted to be accepted as one of them and worked at changing my pattern of speech. Little by little and phrase by phrase I began to adopt the language of the East End of London. Soon I began to feel that I could pass as a Cockney myself, and I felt much more comfortable. However, there was a problem. A lot of their language was not just slang, it was dirty and crude, involving swear words. I love the rich variety of the English language. The choice of just the right word is an exercise of delight. So I was not really tempted to start swearing.

Suddenly one day, while I was laying a wooden floor upstairs, I dropped a box of nails down between the joists, and they scattered on the floor below. Without a thought, the word came out. "Damn!" I said. Everyone stopped work. There was a moment of silence and a laugh or two. The men seemed embarrassed. Any one of them would have sworn loud and long if it had happened to him, but nobody had heard me speak that way. Then somebody said, "He's catching on." And they laughed and got back to work. I went downstairs to pick up my nails.

I really learned something that day. I was amazed that the men had noticed. It also seemed to me that they were embarrassed for me, as if they sensed that I had caught myself off guard and would be ashamed. I was indeed ashamed, and I don't think it happened again.

I had learned that the world is always watching and that people accept for you the standard that you set for yourself. I also learned that I must have allowed myself to absorb a word into my own inner self that I wished I had rejected. I would not and could not have come out with some of the other words that I was hearing all day, because they never became part of my thinking, even at the subconscious level. They had never been accepted by the villi of my spiritual intestines.

I think that my experience with the box of nails taught me that words or ideas that we absorb, even under protest, have a way of coming out under stress and revealing the defilement that we have allowed to accumulate. Jesus said that it is not what we eat that defiles, but what comes out from inside. It can't come out unless it is already inside.

HIDDEN POISON IN THE FOOD

In the last chapter, we talked about the body's incredible ability to filter out impurities and protect us from harmful influences. However, there are subtle poisons that may deceive our defensive guards and get into our bloodstream, where they may destroy us. Dirty stuff can get inside, past the body's defenses.

This suggests that eating a mixed diet is not without danger. It is not without its risks and requires that we are wise about what we take into our bodies.

Our family used to go up into the mountains in the summer in India. We went far away from shops and hospitals. This was good for all of us. There was a lot of physical exercise and a minimum of responsibility.

We enjoyed collecting bamboo shoots and other wild vegetables to eat. One day we collected mushrooms. We thought we knew enough botany to distinguish good mushrooms from bad mushrooms, and we took a batch back to the cabin and cooked them ourselves to add to the feast. They tasted great.

Within half an hour we knew we had made a mistake. What looked like good mushrooms were actually poisonous fungi. We started hallucinating. A trivial object, like a spoon, suddenly seemed to be of enormous significance and beauty. When our daughter asked for a banana, my wife could not think what a banana was. We began to lose our balance. This was just the beginning, and we knew there was a lot more undigested mushroom in our guts that had not yet been absorbed. In a panic we knew we had to rid our bodies of the poison if we were to save our lives.

My wife managed to vomit by putting her fingers down her throat. The rest of us had to drink salt water, and the children soon threw up. I didn't. I took more salt, but my stomach remained at peace. I began to feel I was doomed to absorb poison and die a lonely death on the mountain. Suddenly I felt the muscle of my diaphragm contract, and then my abdomen pulled in. I ran to join the others, leaned across the bath, relaxed before the irresistible contractions. I felt the glorious rush, the cataract of acid soup. My life was saved!

None of us has forgotten that day. One or two of the children have sworn off mushrooms for life. Most of us still look carefully at any mushrooms we buy and still more carefully at those we might gather from the wild. Now that the children are all grown up they look back with gratitude to the foresight of the Creator who designed a stomach that has a reverse gear.

Yes, God designed us with many guards and checkpoints. We can reject food by smell before we eat it or by taste after it enters our mouth, when we can spit it out. We can even reverse the movements of our gut if poison passes the first barriers. Once beyond the stomach, we have villi that know how to screen most things that would harm us. But in spite of all that, we can still be deceived into absorbing harmful chemicals.

DISCHARGE THOSE WASTES

Thus far we have considered the challenge of a mixed diet of solid food mainly from the point of view of intake. We are thankful that we have a God-given digestive system that screens what we take in and absorbs only what is good food.

Digestion has a second responsibility, and that is to *reject* what is left over and get rid of it. Otherwise we do not remain healthy, physically or spiritually.

In the lower part of the bowels, there comes a stage where all that can be used has been absorbed, and the residue is harmful or just completely indigestible. At this point it could be sent out, but it is floating in so much fluid that a lot of water would be lost with it. So the lowest segment of bowel has the important job of extracting as much water as possible and taking it back into the body to be used again at the upper end of the bowel when the next meal comes down.

At this low level the epithelium is not looking for nourishment so much as taking care to avoid absorbing the toxins that are part of the residue of the digestive process. If food residues remain a long time in the gut, they begin to putrefy and become toxic. The lower bowel moves efficiently to conserve the water and to stimulate the elimination of the waste.

However, if we ignore the signals of our bodies, the stimulation becomes increasingly faint. Soon we are chronically constipated. Physically, we are uncomfortable; we begin to suffer from other health problems.

The same principle holds true in the spiritual world. If the urgings of your conscience are ignored, elimination of the toxic and useless elements that we have taken in will slow down or cease. We will no longer enjoy spiritual health. Food for the spiritual adult is that which you go out and get for yourself. It is not preselected. Out there in the real world, if you are going to be a follower of Jesus, you are going to meet good and evil. Good things and bad things are going to be mixed into your daily diet, but you have God's gift of a spiritual digestion that can discriminate. It can choose to absorb the good and to reject the bad and the unnecessary.

I feel strongly about the neglect of our spiritual capacity to reject the evil in our spiritual and social environment. There are two dangers to which we Christians are prone, especially in our culture today. One is, having recognized how much of evil there is in our social environment—in business, in education, in entertainment, in politics—we may respond by saying that this is no place for a Christian. We may seek a purer atmosphere. We may stay home and pray, avoiding the kind of contacts that may contaminate. We try to keep ourselves "unpolluted" from the world. The world, as a consequence, cannot hear the gospel through us.

The second danger is that we accept the need to go out into the world and become involved. We get our hands dirty doing good things for needy people, but we forget the need to discriminate. We no longer actively reject what we know to be evil. We begin to absorb the evil and the good, and soon it affects our spiritual life and our witness.

WITH LOVE ... SIGNED THE DEVIL

Spiritual taste and smell may be deceived as well. It would be easy to resist temptation if it came labeled "from the Devil." His trick is to make evil taste good, to mix it with honey for sweetness and spices for excitement.

Earlier I talked about the inability of children to discriminate what they should watch on television. But adult Christians often have difficulty practicing discrimination in watching TV because programs are calculated to attract us. We find ourselves accepting the hidden assumptions that in other settings we would reject as wrong. Television has become a source of food for the mind and the window through which we view the events of the world and make judgments, not just about events, but about the lifestyles behind them.

Television contains some good nourishment that is mixed in with food additives that are like addictive drugs. The food is served by attractive waiters and waitresses; the atmosphere is comfortable, and music is piped in so that time passes by unnoticed. In contrast the real world strikes a jarring note.

It's easy to forget that the television industry is funded and planned by sponsors who want to profit from your addiction. Of course no one is going to tell you directly that you should change your priorities, become hedonist, and respond to any temptation that comes your way. That would be too obvious. Instead they dish out a constant diet of images that subtly communicate the message that you need more and *more* things to serve and please you and that if you worship at the shrine of greed and pleasure you also will enjoy life more.

Is it possible for a Christian digestion to accept such a diet and remain healthy? Are we perceptive enough to absorb the good and reject the harmful and hidden poisons?

JUST SAY NO

The food that affects us spiritually is not limited to what we take in at a deliberate meal. It's the sum total of the mental impressions we allow to seep into our consciousness during the day. If our conversation is with godly or good people, then we may be built up spiritually. If we choose to keep company with those who are self-centered, some of their ideas and values will become part of our thinking. The difference between the influence of television and that of our relationships is that in our relationships we can object to harmful views and open a discussion. Not so with TV. There seems no point in saying no out loud in the middle of a program. But the alternative is to be passive and to allow mental and emotional food from Hollywood to become our spiritual diet.

I write passionately because I have lived long enough to have a clear before-and-after perspective on television. I believe it has a negative influence. My mother was one of eleven children, and I had about forty first cousins and countless second cousins. To my knowledge none of us has ever gone through a divorce. Doubtless there was tension and unhappiness between spouses from time to time, but we viewed divorce as unthinkable. Because divorce was not considered an option, we had to find other ways to resolve our differences.

Today, even in the church, families are breaking up. Children are shuffled between homes. Counseling is booming. Why have families lost their sense of security and happiness? What has changed? The Bible hasn't. Men and women haven't; they still have the same hormones. The change I see is that worldly attitudes have crept into the church.

How did this happen? Where did these attitudes creep in? Television. The window from the entertainment industry is wide open in almost every home, and we have not realized its danger nor have we devised a secure filter that admits the good and screens out the bad. The sad thing is that not only is our Christian witness being hurt but we are losing our joy.

We put instant personal gratification and short-term happiness first. In our homes we are acting out the situations we see on the screen. The food may taste sweet as it goes in, but it has us deceived. Once inside it behaves like mushroom poison. It creates hallucinations of beauty but causes loss of balance and loss of our heads' control of our bodies. Beware!

THE GENUINE ARTICLE

In India we were constantly faced with problems of malnutrition because the poor couldn't afford the variety of foods they needed to stay healthy. So the biochemists and public health nurses at our medical college studied diets to see how to make it possible for the poor to eat well enough to fight disease.

I was fascinated by one of their early findings: the very poor were often better nourished than the moderately poor. In our part of India most people were farmers. Some owned land, and others worked as coolies for the landowners. Most people in the system could afford to buy food in the marketplace, and rice was usually plentiful. In the more remote villages, many people could not afford much rice and had no irrigated land. They grew a crop called ragi that did not need much water and would grow on poor soil. Ragi was a rather coarse, small brown grain that was despised by those who could afford rice. Most rice was "polished" before being sold and was nice to look at and white and soft when cooked. The very poor had to make do with unpolished rice when they could afford rice at all.

Our nutritionists and biochemists found that ragi contained a wonderful array of vitamins and minerals and was a healthful food. Rice was mainly starch, but it was a more complete food if it was eaten unpolished. In fact, rice polishings were prescribed as a good food supplement for malnourished patients.

When these findings came out, Margaret and I took to serving ragi ourselves at home and for the children. We bought it rather finely milled so it did not feel gritty, but it was whole ragi. When visitors came to our house we enjoyed seeing their looks of puzzlement as they saw ragi being served—"beggar's food." Today when I visit India I always bring home a bag of ragi. Margaret mixes it in with the dough when she makes our multigrain whole-meal bread.

Our nutritionists also tested many plants that grew wild around the villages in south India. At that time we were seeing many cases of keratomalacia from local villages. This is a cause of childhood blindness that results from ordinary conjunctivitis, or pinkeye. Conjunctivitis is common in most countries. It does not usually threaten sight, but if it affects a child whose eyes have become dry and dangerously weakened by vitamin

A deficiency, it causes devastating corneal ulceration. Within a few days that little child may be rendered hopelessly blind. This used to be tragically common around Vellore.

The body can build vitamin A from most dark green leafy vegetables. Spinach, kale, and broccoli are rich sources. But these were not grown in the villages near us in India. There was, however, a class of what the village people called weeds that grew freely around the houses, known as kiri. Kiri doesn't taste like our best hybrid spinach, but a person can develop a taste for it if it is used in imaginative recipes. Our public health nurses educated the people about kiri, and soon these vulnerable toddlers were being protected from blindness. Keratomalacia has become quite uncommon around Vellore now.

THE JOY OF SIMPLE FOODS

Americans don't have to struggle to find food that contains what we need for healthy bodies. Here we have access to an array of good and simple foods. But our children may have their tastes perverted by the food industry before they have an opportunity to learn the quieter ecstasies of real food as God made it. I urge parents in city environments to try hard to compensate for the deprivation that their children suffer as a result. Make sure that their developing tastes have time to learn the joys of simple food. This, of course, involves eating right yourself.

One of the things that endeared Mahatma Gandhi to his followers was that he never asked them to do anything that he was not willing to do himself. He lived in an extended village in a simple one-room hut. One day a woman came, bringing her little son, and asked Gandhi a question. "Bapu," she said, using his nickname, "I am having a problem with my little son. I cannot stop him chewing sugar cane. I take it away from him and scold him, but he goes away and gets some more and chews it in private. His teeth are getting bad already. If you tell him, Bapu, I think he will stop. He respects you." The Mahatma told her to go away and come back a week later, and he would do what he could.

After a week the woman came back with her son, and Mahatma called the boy to him and spoke to him kindly and sternly, warning him of the problems he would have with tooth decay and telling him that he must give up chewing sugar cane. The boy was impressed and promised to give it up. The mother thanked Mahatma and turned to leave. Then she turned back, "Bapu, you could have told him all that last week. Why did you tell us to come back?

"No, Madam, I could not have told him last week, because last week I had not given up chewing sugar cane myself."

Many of the temptations used by the devil to spoil our spiritual lives are things that, like sugar, were designed by God for our good. C. S. Lewis pointed out in *Screwtape Letters* that the devil has never invented any pleasure himself. He depends on misuse of the real pleasures that God intended for our enjoyment in the context of a life lived within his guidelines.

Let's be on guard lest we be deceived.

CHAPTER 11

The Guardians of the Gate

It was excellently said of that philosopher, that there was a wall or parapet of teeth set in our mouth, to restrain the petulancy of our words.

~ BEN JOHNSON, *EXPLORATA: LINQUA SAPIENTIS*

The tongue breaketh bone,
Though itself have none.

~ PROVERBS OF ALFRED, AD 1425

Our amazing bodies, with their economy of function, often use a single organ for more than one task. The same nose that detects the fragrance of the orange blossom also takes in the air we breathe. Ears that hear the sound of the nightingale also give us the gift of balance. The critically important mouth has many tasks as well.

As adults, we generally talk and eat without conscious effort. This makes it easy for us to overlook one of the most important members of the body—the tongue.

The book of James has a chapter on the difficulty of taming the tongue, calling it an "unruly evil." Such language seems a little harsh for an organ that obeys the brain so precisely. People often speak of wanting to bite their tongue when they've said something unkind. Yet they would be better off praying for control of their thoughts so that their minds will instruct their tongues to speak kind words. When I want to speak, my conscious mind thinks of what I want to say, and the nerves that control my tongue make it dance, dart, and twist as it gives shape to the sounds that come from my vocal cords. It turns them into vowels and consonants that make up the unique sound of my voice. Every person uses his tongue just a little differently, manipulating the common sounds of his tongue with the music of his own distinctive vocal signature.

My son Christopher, who had been living in Hawaii for some years, was flipping the channels of his television set when he heard a couple of words in passing. "That's Dad!" he called out to his wife, as he tuned back to the station. He found a program on leprosy in which I had been demonstrating a case. He had no reason to think I would be on TV, but even in those fleeting seconds, he recognized my voice.

What a tribute to the mechanisms in the brain! Have you ever seen a soundtrack of speech on a computer screen? If so, think of all those spikes of variable size that record all the sounds of speech. How many neurons in the brain does it take to store the soundtrack of the way one person speaks, so that it can be distinguished from the same words spoken by anybody else? This memory is stored in the brain, as one might store facts in the archives of a library, and the brain has instant access to it. In Hawaii just two or three words, springing out of years of history, instantly identified their origin. The routines of my tongue are so disciplined, they are able to produce my words with the same inflections as they did years ago when Christopher was a child. I couldn't begin to tell my tongue which filaments of muscle to contract to make this happen. But a million of my nerve cells know every twist and flick of my tongue and can produce them at a moment's notice, exactly the way they did thirty years ago.

A SLIP OF THE TONGUE

But our tongues do more than help us speak. When we eat our food, we don't think about what we're doing. Chewing requires no conscious thought about the tongue's whereabouts, except, perhaps, when the tongue needs to quickly get food out of the way so it can shift gears and switch to its other job: talking. (Don't talk with your mouth full, Johnny!)

My teeth are hard and sharp, and they can cut and crush most of the things that enter my mouth. They can't feel the subtle differences between a piece of steak and my nerve-filled tongue. Like hammers and millstones, they come crashing closely together, cutting and grinding everything that comes between them. My tongue lives in much greater danger than would be permitted by any code of occupational safety, but I rarely give it a thought.

In this deadly environment, the tongue scoops up unchewed food and pushes it in between my teeth—with no time to spare. My tongue has maybe a quarter of a second to find a glob of food and another eighth of a second to push it between the teeth before they come crashing down. Then, even more quickly, it has to get out of the way, to safety. If in escaping the left-hand row of teeth it panics and jumps to the right, it will get pulverized by the teeth in the right-hand row.

The instant pain we feel when we bite our tongue keeps us from closing our jaws any further. Its warning may not be quick enough to prevent the tongue being hurt and bruised, but it's nearly always in time to stop it being mangled like a piece of chewed-up food.

Once we bite our tongue, eating slows down considerably, and it even hurts to talk. The body, as if repentant for carelessly accepting the tongue's dangerous working conditions, now gives priority to protecting this wounded member until it is healed.

A ROVING SENSOR

The tongue has exquisite sensitivity of touch and taste. It defends the stomach and all the passages beyond. It can't analyze the nature of the food, but it does screen it all for anything that might be harmful or unwanted.

Think about what happens at a meal when people are eating cherries or fish with tiny bones. Lively chatter ceases as people concentrate on finding the pit or bone in their mouths. Moving quickly in the dark, sensing textures blended in the matrix of the food, the tongue tip locates and isolates the unwanted item. Its pursuit is as relentless as a sheepdog that is isolating one sheep from a moving flock. Once the prisoner is captured, the tongue guides it and delivers it to the lips to be unobtrusively discarded.

I'm even more amazed at what I've observed about the tongue's sensitivity through my patients with leprosy. Leprosy destroys the nerves of touch and pain and sometimes leaves patients unable to see, or even to feel, what they hold in their hands. Yet their tongues almost always retain sensation. I have seen a patient dress himself, using only his tongue to identify a shirt by texture from an undershirt and to locate a button hole or Velcro patch along its edge. What an inspiration to see the human spirit refusing to accept defeat!

The lively movements of the tongue are lubricated from glands inside the mouth. When we need water, the tongue is the first part of our body to sense our need. Lubrication stops and our tongue feels dry. People who have almost died from thirst remember vividly how their dry, swollen tongue stuck to the roof of their mouth.

Historical accounts of crucifixion emphasize the swollen, dried tongue as a terrible feature of that barbaric practice. David gives a prophetic account of Jesus' sufferings on the cross: "My strength is dried up like a potsherd, and my tongue sticks to the roof of my mouth" (Psalm 22:15). These images conjure up a vivid picture of Jesus crying out, "I'm thirsty" and underscore the bitter irony when He was given vinegar instead of water.

In the next Psalm, the Twenty-third, Jesus is pictured again, now as our shepherd leading us beside still waters, ensuring that we never have to experience a dry tongue. Jesus then prepares a table before us. Enemies may still be around us, but we feast with our Lord and dwell in His house forever. I'm not going to speculate about what will be on the table at the marriage feast of the lamb, but I'm sure there will be water. How else could our tongues sing praises continually and eat our feast at the same time?

CHEW ON IT

But in writing about the wonders of the tongue, I don't mean to cast the teeth in the role of villains. We need them. Our teeth make it possible for us to move from milk to solid food as they begin the process of digestion by chewing up our food. Our teeth are destined to eat a variety of food, so the front teeth are fairly sharp for tearing, and the molars further back are able to grind soft foods and fruits and grains.

Teeth are essential for anyone who sets out to tackle solid food, especially if it is of uncertain origin. People sometimes laugh at a person who is gullible, saying, "He swallowed the story whole—hook, line, and sinker." The word *gullible* refers to a person who is ready to swallow without analysis, without chewing it over first.

It's not good for our stomachs if we swallow large chunks of food which then have to be analyzed by chemical juices. People who make a habit of taking meals on the run don't take time to chew their food properly, and they swallow half-chewed food. This is a disdainful way to treat the digestive system that is their inheritance. They may not realize it, but such treatment is likely to result in chronic indigestion in the future. The more we chew our food, the easier it is to digest. This is true in the spiritual sense as well.

My wife and I go to a church where we are served great spiritual meals at our Sunday services. I sometimes take notes, but while I'm writing down one point, I sometimes miss the next. So we take home a tape of the sermon. Believe it or not, it's sometimes better the second time around! I can stop the tape and replay something a couple of times until I am sure I can digest and absorb it.

Besides aiding in digestion, another advantage of chewing on a piece of food is that it allows us to discover whether something bad was hidden in the food. We can spit it out rather than swallow it. Chewing helps us be selective. If a Christian is to go out into the world, he or she must be on guard not to accept ideas or suggestions at face value. The same is true of doctrine within the church. Paul, having spoken about the need to grow up within the body of Christ, says, "Then [having grown up] we will no longer be infants,... blown here and there by every wind of teaching and by the cunning and craftiness of men" (Ephesians 4:14). Paul is saying, in effect, "Don't swallow any teaching whole; chew it over and discriminate before you swallow." This theme comes up again and again in advice to the young churches as new ideas are presented to them. The action of teeth is important for solid food, whether it is physical or spiritual.

The teeth are unique in that they project through the skin that covers all the rest of the body. They protrude through what is really a wound in the lining of the mouth, but a seal between tooth and skin keeps infection out of the socket. Periodontal membrane is unique for this purpose. This sealing membrane has another important quality. It is sensitive to pressure on the tooth. If a person has an irregular tooth or one that has been filled or capped a little high, the membrane quickly knows that at every bite it is the first to feel pressure and that it takes an unfair share of the load. The body is informed of the problem and instructs all the muscles that move the lower jaw to shift it around and try biting in various positions until the high pressure is relieved and all teeth take an equal share. This sometimes results in quite an awkward way of chewing, and some little jaw muscles have to work hard to save the tooth from the overload that otherwise would make for painful inflammation in its socket. When these jaw muscles are overworked, they complain and sometimes go into painful spasms.

A patient may complain of headaches or pain in the face, diagnosed as migraine or neuralgia, and may take a lot of drugs to relieve chronic pain. A good dentist will test the bite and then grind down the prominent tooth just a fraction. Presto! All the muscles relax. The jaws bite normally, all the pains are relieved, and life returns to normal.

When dentists find that teeth don't fit because one hard-headed member is too prominent, they use the word *proud*. "This denture is a little proud at the first premolar. Just grind it down a bit, where I have marked it."

I sometimes wish it were as easy to deal with prominent and hard-headed members of the church. They cause strain among all the other members, who try to avoid giving offense.

No wonder the Lord hates pride, the first of all the deadly sins, and how we need to pray that if our own ego rises too high, the grace of God will grind us down a bit, until we fit in with our fellow members, and we work together in harmony.

The enamel of the tooth is so hard and dense that it cannot have a blood supply. It is layered over the softer core of the tooth, which we call dentine, and has a pulp cavity carrying nerves and blood vessels.

Teeth last longer than any other part of the body. In ancient remains, where even skeletons have crumbled away, the teeth may remain and tell us something of the way that person lived and ate when alive. If the molars have worn flat, we can suppose there has been constant chewing or grinding on raw grains or raw blubber, as in Eskimo lands. If teeth are broken, we suspect there has been fighting. The presence of cavities may indicate that this person lived after sugar was refined and therefore help scientists estimate the age of the skeleton. Or perhaps the cavities may have been caused by a lack of calcium in the soil.

No matter what the cause, tooth decay brings helpless misery. Those who have instant access to dental help hardly know the throbbing agony that can come with tooth decay. The swelling of infection and inflammation, locked up in a cavity of bone, produces pain that can override every thought and action. It's worse because it is out of reach.

I remember my parents extracting teeth from people in pain, at any time of day or night. They did it on the doorsteps of our house, under trees, while on trek, or on the threshold of a village hut. People would travel across the mountain with a cloth wrapped around their face. All they knew was that the missionary was never without dental forceps and was always willing to help. There was no anesthetic; there was no dental chair, only a rock or termite mound. The offending tooth was identified, and the forceps were applied. A quick twist of the wrist, a grunt, or perhaps a scream of pain, and it was over. The tooth was carried home as a trophy and as a signal to others that there was relief to be had on the other side of the mountain.

My parents gave us children extra calcium to try to forestall decay for us. It didn't help much. I personally had a series of cavities develop during World War II while I was on double duty as a senior medical student and as an assistant in emergency surgery on bomb victims in the London Blitz. It was too difficult to make or keep dental appointments when I was on constant call, so I fixed up my room in my hospital quarters to mend my own teeth.

I had taken a course in basic dentistry. I fixed my shaving mirror on my dressing table and borrowed two dental mirrors and a handful of drill bits. I had oil of cloves and zinc oxide. Sitting in front of my mirror and using my left hand to hold a dental mirror and also to retract my cheek, I twirled the drill bits between my right finger and thumb to prepare my cavities for filling. I needed no anesthetic; I knew exactly when my drill was near a tender spot, and I had direct control. I had several sessions on each tooth, using temporary fillings of cotton soaked in oil of cloves between. The final filling was a stiff paste of zinc oxide and oil of cloves, pressed in and polished flush with the tooth.

I did four such fillings, intended to last just until I had time to visit a dentist. But I forgot them and years later had them replaced while I was working in Beirut, Lebanon. The fillings were still in good condition, and no decay had been left behind. My Lebanese dentist was almost speechless when I explained how the fillings had been done. (I'm not recommending that anyone follow my example—crazy things can happen during a war!)

GUARDIANS OF DOCTRINE

In the body of Christ, we need members who, like teeth, will make sure that we are all being fed good food, that our teaching is without error or heresy. Their job is to be critical of teaching to make sure it doesn't contain fragments of harmful ideas.

There are few functions in the body of Christ that require more care and attention than the interaction of hard members and soft. The example of Jesus Christ leads us to love sinners and to feel pain with those who hurt. That doesn't mean we have to adopt or condone the philosophy that has led to the hurt in the first place, however. Teeth are symbolic of uncompromising attitudes in the defense of truth. The lips symbolize love and a kiss and a welcome. Yet they are both functions of the same body.

A current problem within the church that calls for the delicate balance between judgment and compassion is homosexuality. Our "teeth" make a harsh analysis, but a biblical one. They recognize the danger of departing from scriptural standards and allow no softening of the attitudes of the church. In their role as guardians of doctrine they tell us not to accept what may spread and harm the church. Our softer parts may feel the hurt of those who feel criticized and stigmatized and may want to offer mercy and love. These two contrasting functions of the body of Christ are not incompatible. In fact, either one may be wrong without something of the other.

People debating this issue can take sides in a heated argument and lose all sense of fellowship and love. There's no easy way to resolve real confrontation in a church. In the body of Christ, the decisions must be made by our head, which is Christ. It is our responsibility to get together and pray. Pray first for loyalty and harmony within the body. Pray for wisdom to know what is right in the sight of God and what is going to be good for the body as a whole. We may come to realize that while it is always right to show compassion and love to those outside the body of Christ, that doesn't mean they should be invited into intimate fellowship with members of His body unless there's a change of heart.

Let us be aware how teeth can cause pain and resolve that those of us who are sensitive may actively seek to prevent the confrontations that might destroy our fellowship.

A DANGEROUS CROSSROAD

The mouth is a great junction, or crossroads, between food, water, and air. When we have a cold and our nose is stuffed, we have to open our mouth and take a breath, whether or not we have food in our mouth. This may be considered bad manners, but it's a practical way to stay alive while we eat. Our bodies can't wait long to breathe, and sometimes we have to breathe before our food is ready to be swallowed. If our nose is blocked, we have no option but to breathe through our mouth.

Every mouthful of food, however, comes to a critical junction at which air goes one way and food another. This is a point of even greater danger than that of the tongue; it is a matter of life and death. Food swallowed down the windpipe may choke off the passage of air to the lungs and kill within five minutes. If the food gets down to the lungs, it may kill within days or weeks due to the development of pneumonia and consolidation of segments of the lungs.

As in every part of the body, when there is a possibility of danger, God has designed us with safety devices of extraordinary efficiency. The vocal cords, which are the narrow gateway to the lungs, are tough and stringy bands with special muscles to narrow or widen the opening and to tighten the strings to tune the voice. It is here that most emergencies occur. A small object can block the opening, and a drop of fluid can trickle through to irritate the windpipe or the lungs.

It is too dangerous to let food and fluid flow across this musical instrument that serves also as an emergency door. So there is another set of muscles that swings into action as soon as bells announce a swallow on the way. Two little cartilages, clothed in muscle and lined with membrane skin, swing across the voice box and seal it shut. By the time the food arrives at this gullet, there is only one pathway ahead. The vocal cords are hidden and protected. As soon as the food and water have passed, the muscles swing apart, and breath and voice are free to breathe and sing.

As with so many situations where life and death depend upon the choice of when and how a muscle works, the conscious brain is not trusted to control the choice. Deep in the reflex patterns of subconscious knowledge, long before a baby is allowed to leave its mother's womb, a powerful discipline is built into nerves and muscle cells.

As soon as food or fluid approaches, the never-sleeping cells that rim the glottis swing the gates shut and keep them closed until the stream flows by. This happens so smoothly that consciousness is not disturbed. If something should go wrong, if just two drops of milk should get there before the gates have shut and trickle through the larynx towards the lungs, then all priorities change. Nothing else matters. People in the line of fire had better take cover, because the chest and the diaphragm concentrate all their power to blast explosive coughs of air upward through the larynx and out through the mouth. They carry with them every scrap of food or fluid that may be in their way. Coughing goes on until the exclusive pathway of the breath is clear.

So we are protected. Food and air may mix in the mouth. We may talk and breathe with our mouth full, violating good manners. But once we start to swallow, we have to obey the policeman who stands guard at the gateway of the breath, and his word is law.

Why is the guardian so strict, and why are the rules of entry to the lungs so unbending? Because the gullet marks the parting of two completely different ways by which we absorb what the body needs. The air we breathe brings us oxygen, an essential ingredient for life that has to be absorbed directly into the bloodstream. Food gets into the bloodstream eventually, but first it has to go through a rigorous process of digestion. So breath uses a different pathway and is permitted a degree of intimacy with the blood that would never be allowed to any other essential element, solid or liquid.

Once past all barriers, incoming breath flows on into the lungs themselves, into a huge area of tiny folded air sacs. Here the air comes into an intimacy with the blood that is as close as it is possible to be without actual mixing. Tiny blood capillaries, having shed the outer garments of muscle they had on their way into the lungs, now nakedly present the corpuscles they carry to the oxygen of the air, with only a gossamer membrane between. In that close encounter, both air and blood share and exchange their gases. The oxygen of the air restores the depleted oxygen of the red cells of the blood, while the carbon dioxide of the blood is unloaded into the air.

If gas comes in with the breath, it becomes part of the bloodstream as the blood flows on toward the heart. When medicines are given by mouth, it may take many minutes or hours for them to reach the body through the gut. However, if breathed into the lungs, these same medicines become intruders that may affect the whole body in only seconds. The Creator, who designed the lungs for instant intimacy with air to use the oxygen and rid the body of pollutants, knew also the dangers of quick acceptance of what might be harmful. That's why we cough and sneeze and why, instinctively, we get away from smoke and dust and dislike polluted air.

The smoker, whose dependence on nicotine has made him or her feel insecure under stress, lights up a cigarette when pressure builds. If you watch, you will observe that the effect is immediate. The first deep drag on the cigarette, and the smoker begins to relax. Confidence is restored. The result is so dramatic that it's easy to assume that the cigarette is a good thing. Of course there would be no need for nicotine if the normal chemistry of the brain had not been altered by the earlier nicotine habit. The nicotine "high" is only a brief return to what would have been normal all the time if the habit had never started.

For many years the most famous of the early newscasters on television was sponsored by Chesterfield cigarettes. He would conclude his news program by lighting up a cigarette while the name of the brand was on the screen. He immediately relaxed. The image of peace was so vivid that the sales of Chesterfields increased enormously and boosted the profits of the company.

I'm told that when that broadcaster was dying of lung cancer and struggling for every breath, he asked to appear on the same TV program so that others might see the long-term results of what he had previously advertised. His request was refused.

DON'T LET YOUR GAG REFLEX
GO TO SLEEP

In the Bible, breath and wind are used quite frequently as symbols of the Spirit. Jesus himself described the Spirit of God as like the wind, and after He rose from the dead and appeared to the disciples, He breathed on them, saying "receive the Holy Spirit."

The analogy of Spirit as breath reminds us that it's the Spirit that mediates real peace, not the spurious peace of a "high" on drugs. In John 14:26–27 Jesus first introduces His disciples to the Spirit, the Comforter, who is to come, and continues, "Peace I leave with you; my peace I give you. I do not give to you as the world gives. Do not let your hearts be troubled" (v. 27).

The Bible urges us to "test the spirits" (1 John 4:1). The danger of false spirits is not that they look or smell poisonous; it's that they seem so innocuous. They use the name of Jesus, but they deny His divinity. In order to foster church growth, they preach a gospel that doesn't require any major changes in the way we choose to live. It was a false spirit that suggested to Jesus that He could gain a much wider audience if he used the authority of Satan to further the gospel.

Sometimes a throat specialist needs to have a careful look at the vocal cords. He may spray an anesthetic around the area to prevent you from gagging as he puts his mirror where he needs it. As you leave he tells you not to eat or drink anything for a while because your gag reflex has been put to sleep. The doorway to your lungs is open. This is good advice. In your spiritual life, too, never let your gag reflex go to sleep. Always be ready to test the spirits. Your breath is where you are most vulnerable.

In today's culture, some of our greatest dangers are not the outright poisons that one might face from snakes or poisonous berries. We need to be afraid of the poisons that take over our mind and alter our thinking. Alcohol and drugs alter our perception of reality and truth. Alcohol, heroin, or crack all share the same miserable characteristics. They work by taking control of the highest faculties of the mind and brain, changing the perception of what is good and what is bad. They introduce a short circuit into the experience of pleasure so that the subject may begin to enjoy the things that destroy it. They not only change the moral sense, but the physical and mental. They send new orders to the guardians at the gate. They order the openings of the gate into the lungs and allow inhalation of dangerous gases.

Carbon monoxide is one of the gases that is dangerous to life, not because it is addictive, but because it has no warning smell. The guardians let it through. Methane and carbon monoxide were so dangerous in coal mines in England in the last century that miners used to take a live canary into the mines with them. If the bird died, all the miners got out of the mine as fast as they could.

God is calling members of His own body, the church, to become more committed and more alert at the gateway to the lungs, at the place where the devil would like to find acceptance for today's evil spirits. We have lost enough of our children to convince us that the danger is real. Evil spirits are skilled deceivers, so watch out! The apostle says: "Be self-controlled and alert. Your enemy the devil prowls around like a roaring lion looking for someone to devour" (1 Peter 5:8). Today, he may be less like a lion and more like a seductive vapor or powder or fluid, but we need the same vigilance.

CHAPTER 12

Give Us This Day Our Daily Bread

The stomach sets us to work.

~ GEORGE ELIOT, *FELIX HOLT*

There is no reason that the senseless Temples of God should abound in riches, and the living Temples of the Holy Spirit starve for hunger.

~ ETHELWOLD, BISHOP OF WINCHESTER, WHEN SELLING THE
GOLD AND SILVER VESSELS OF HIS CHURCH DURING A FAMINE
IN AD 980 IN WILLIAM CAMDEN, *REMAINS OF BRITAIN*

After having lived for most of my life in India where many Christians struggle to eke out a meager existence, I have given a lot of thought to this question: Does God feed the hungry?

It's true that many passages in Scripture, if taken at face value, seem to suggest that if we have faith in God we don't need to be concerned about where our meals are going to come from—that God will provide. Jesus tells His disciples not to worry about what they will eat or what they will wear. "Life is more than food . . . Consider the ravens: They do not sow or reap, . . . yet God feeds them. And how much more valuable you are than birds! . . . Seek first his kingdom, . . . and all these things will be given to you" (Luke 12:23–24; Matthew 6:33).

David says that "the lions may grow weak and hungry, but those who seek the Lord lack no good thing" (Psalm 34:10).

There are many stories in the Bible where God does provide food for the hungry: He sent manna and quail to the children of Israel as they crossed the wilderness to find the Promised Land (Exodus 16). Jesus fed more than five thousand hungry people by multiplying loaves and fishes (John 6).

Not long after this miracle, the crowds sought out Jesus with broad hints that they would follow Him if he kept on giving them more food. Jesus turned the discussion to a spiritual level: "Do not work for food that spoils, but for food that endures to eternal life" (John 6:27).

In this book we've been looking at parallels between the physical human body and the spiritual body of Christ. Sometimes these are obvious, so much so that there's a danger of thinking they're identical. For example, it would appear that God must be referring to both spiritual and physical food when He promises to feed us. But this isn't necessarily so. We need to distinguish the promises that relate to spiritual food from those that relate to physical nourishment.

Paul writes in 2 Thessalonians 3:7–10:

> We were not idle when we were with you, nor did we eat anyone's food without paying for it. On the contrary, we worked night and day, laboring and toiling so that we would not be a burden to any of you. We did this, not because we do not have the right to such help, but in order to make ourselves a model for you to follow . . . We gave you this rule: "If a man will not work, he shall not eat."

These verses refer specifically to physical food—to bread or money for it. Clearly, the New Testament church had a work ethic. They expected members to work for their food if they could and to recognize their responsibility to provide for members who were unable to fend for themselves. But even for the widows and orphans the apostles did not expect any special miracles or "acts of God." Deacons were appointed by the church to organize the sharing out of what the members already had.

Within a healthy physical body every member has access to whatever food the body obtains. However, during starvation a body may allow some tissue—such as fat—to be depleted in order to feed the members that are essential for the body's survival. The body can't create food out of nothing, even when there is need. When it needs food, the body works hard to get it and then shares it according to the need of all its members. This basic principle is also true of spiritual food.

THE HEAVENLY FATHER'S PROVISION

When Jesus said that God fed the birds, He wasn't carrying around a tray of bird seed. None of the hearers thought the ravens depended on Jesus for direct supplies. What, then, did He mean? I think we see the answer as we look at how God, as creator and provider for all of life, has provided each of His species with their own way of obtaining food.

I'm a bird watcher and am constantly amazed and delighted at how various species exercise their unique skills and instincts for survival. I love to see the thrush cock its head to one side as it listens for worms. I can't hear worms, but a thrush can. Its feet can sense vibration, and its exquisite hearing tells it just where to jump for its breakfast.

The acorn woodpecker on the Pacific Coast drills holes in tree trunks and then goes and finds acorns that just fit the hole. It drives the acorns into the holes and leaves them. It repeats the process until hundreds of acorns decorate the trunk of the tree. Later in the year, perhaps in winter, the woodpecker comes back and pecks out its old acorns. By now the acorn and the hole are full of insects, and between insects and acorns the woodpecker gets a balanced meal of protein, carbohydrate, and fat.

My heavenly Father has designed a woodpecker's beak so it can drill holes in wood. He also gave them special fluid suspensions in the skull so that their brains are not vibrated to pieces. He has written programs in the DNA of the acorn woodpecker that translate into an ability to recognize acorns and to know what to do with them and to know that it is better not to eat them fresh but wait until they mature and are infested with insects.

As I watch birds and raccoons and rabbits—even lilies of the field—all exercising their hidden knowledge and skills to find their food and feed their young, I keep thinking, "My heavenly Father feeds them!" He is the source of their wisdom, instinct, and skill. I believe Jesus chose to use the example of His care for His humbler creations so that His disciples would stop worrying about their own food and clothing.

Jesus wants us to be thankful for all the skill and wisdom and instinct that He has lovingly built into us humans. He expects us to use what He has given us for our survival.

Many birds die in an especially cold winter. Even with all the resources God built into them, the struggle for life has been too hard. God doesn't intervene on an individual basis to save the life of a bird—though he feels sadness because all life has its origin in His life. Neither does He usually intervene to save the life of a human being. We die—and this means more to God because men and women carry His image. Even so, God rarely acts directly to change His own physical laws in order to make life easier for one of His children.

However, David tells us, "I was young and now I am old, yet I have never seen the righteous forsaken or their children begging bread" (Psalm 37:25). I, too, have seen God's faithful servants throw themselves on His mercy, asking for help for themselves and their families. And their needs have sometimes been met in ways that give no room for doubt that God intervened to provide for their need.

George Müller's orphanage in England was an amazing enterprise of faith. Müller believed that God was concerned for the orphan children entrusted to his care and that He would provide; for this reason, he wouldn't ask the public for money or food. Again and again the orphanage would come to the end of its food supplies, and staff members would plead with Müller to tell supporters about the urgent need. His response was always to pray. Always—and often just in the nick of time—food or money arrived. It was usually a gift from someone who could not explain why he sent it except he had felt a strong impulse and knew that he had to do it.

THE ORIGINAL WELFARE PROGRAM

And yet such intervention seems to be an exception to how God usually works. How, then, could David say he had *never* seen the righteous forsaken? I've come to believe that David's statement is a testimony to the laws and principles on which the nation of Israel had been built.

The Law of Moses, given to him by God, included detailed instructions about the care of the destitute. Poor farmers were to be given interest-free loans. At harvest time no farmer was allowed to reap the corners or the edges of his field; this was left for the poor to reap. Reapers were to drop handfuls of grain for the gleaners to pick up and take home so that they wouldn't have to beg. Gleaning was hard work and an honorable way for the poor to have food.

Wealthy farmers were forbidden to buy up a number of small family farms and combine them to make big farms. If a farmer did sell his land for cash, such a sale was to be only on a leasing basis, and the land was to be returned to the first owner at the Jubilee year.

This Levitical law had become neglected and broken by the time of Isaiah (Isaiah 5:8). The creation of large farms (or agribusinesses) resulted in degradation of the land. Worse, it created a landless class of people who had nothing to fall back upon except to serve as day laborers to the rich. The prophet Micah proclaimed God's anger against the rich who were making themselves richer and the poor even poorer. (This is happening in the United States today. Our laws and banking practices make it more difficult than ever for small farmers to survive. The gap between rich and poor is widening.)

Some of these Levitical land laws were being observed in David's time and were probably the basis for his saying that he had "never seen the righteous forsaken or their children begging bread." Through these laws God provided for the poor both by creating an honorable way to get food and by ensuring that every family would have ultimate title to some land, at least enough to provide for themselves.

WHAT DOES IT MEAN TO LIVE BY FAITH?

If it's not God's purpose to intervene on a physical basis to satisfy individual needs, is there a scriptural basis for those who choose to live by faith?

When I was growing up in England, there was much discussion in our church about faith missions. My church was part of a small denomination that supported a mission society in India. My parents served in that mission and were supported by a small salary from the funds collected by the individual churches.

During this time the China Inland Mission and the World Evangelization Crusade were founded. Their leaders believed, like George Müller, that they were not to ask people for money; instead, they were to pray that God would provide.

Our little mission society sometimes felt put down when others asked, "Are your missionaries paid, or do they live by faith?" We felt that *all* support came from God's people and that faith was involved whether the mission asked for support directly or simply prayed that God would provide it.

Many missions require that their prospective missionaries raise their own support. This encourages individuals to share in the mission enterprise in a personal way because they know exactly where their money is going and what it is being used for. However, some people have many wealthy friends or can speak well and have no difficulty raising their support, while others, who may be good at what they have set out to do, are shy and ineffective at fundraising.

After being involved with missions all my life, both on the receiving end and on the giving end, I believe the church and mission organizations can work together to meet the needs of foreign missions. Individual local churches need to keep in touch with the needs of their members and missionaries. Members can be a great source of spiritual, emotional, and physical support as they correspond and pray for missionaries. This helps missionaries feel a part of the local church body.

Mission organizations can better provide or raise the funds for big expenses, salaries, buildings, and travel. This kind of interchurch sharing assures missionaries of access to leaders who have experience in the problems of living and working in a different culture.

A SPIRITUAL CO-OP

God's part in His plan for the feeding of mankind is the provision of soil and water and seed and sun. He also designed the laws of biology. Our part is to work with God's raw materials and to be thankful for the harvest. We need also to be good stewards of the earth He left us.

God meets the needs of His own people without altering the laws of nature or of morality; He's chosen to use us as part of His plan, and that means we must keep open the lines of communication between the members of His body. Each one of us needs to obey His will and respond to the needs of other members. Paul was part of a church that emphasized providing support and care for widows and orphans. He also acknowledged, though he himself lived by tent-making, that teachers and preachers needed—and were worthy—of support.

We are to work together in the body of Christ the same way the members of our physical body work together. We all know that carrots contain vitamins that are necessary for good eyesight. However, we don't expect our eyes to dig in the garden and plant carrots or to chew them up and digest them. Other parts of our body pull the carrots, scrape them, and eat them; still others extract from the digested carrots just what is needed by the eyes and sends it to them in solution by arterial express.

God's provision for our needs, both physical and spiritual, calls for our active cooperation and response. When we pray "Give us this day our daily bread," we don't expect it to fall from heaven. Rather we expect God's answer to our prayers in His call to us to work with Him and with others in His body.

I experienced firsthand how God feeds His people through the obedience of members of His body and their willingness to share what He had given them. It was a lesson that has stuck with me my whole life.

It was 1936, and I was trying to decide what kind of mission society I should sign up with. I had enrolled in the Missionary Training Colony in London, England, a Bible college that also focused on helping prepare potential missionaries to live simply. One important aspect of our training was the annual six-week trek. We were divided into groups of about twelve, each with a staff member who shared the experience with us. We carried a bell tent and cooking materials in a two-wheel cart that we pulled along with us. We marched during the day and preached in the open air or by invitation in little church halls at night. At night we pitched our tent in a local field, or we slept on the floor of the church hall where we had been preaching.

In our briefings we had been told that this was a "faith" enterprise. We would trust the Lord to provide our food and other needs along the way. We were not allowed to ask for anything. This was to be a journey of faith.

This was my first trek, and I had doubts about whether we really needed to be entirely dependent on gifts we might receive along the way, when some of us could probably afford to buy some food of our own. I voiced my questions to a fellow trekker, and we decided to bring along some of our own money as a reserve and a way to enjoy an occasional treat.

By about the third day, rations were becoming tight, and Philip and I looked at each other and slipped off to buy an ice cream. We got back to camp just in time for the evening prayer meeting. We prayed for those to whom we'd be speaking, and then the prayers turned to the group's needs. We told God about our need for food and money and asked that He direct His people to meet our needs. Again, Philip and I glanced at each other, though not with amusement. We knew we were not in fellowship. This wasn't just fun—it was cheating, and we found it impossible to join the others in prayer.

That was the last time we ate on our own. I sent my money home; my step was lighter as I enjoyed the fellowship of the team. We were functioning as the body of Christ. As in our physical bodies, if one cell is well fed, then all cells share a sense of well being. One cell doesn't go hungry unless all cells are short of food. One cell or one group of cells does not have a secret source of food. In the physical body, such a cell is called a cancer.*

One day our housekeeper of the week told us we were out of money. No gifts had come in, and we had just enough food for one good meal. We agreed that we would eat well that evening and leave only coffee for breakfast.

We were up early, as we had about fourteen miles to our next stop. We gave thanks for breakfast and drank our coffee. We washed out the mugs and packed the empty food storage box. Then, harnessed to the long ropes, we began our march for the day.

There was not much traffic on that country road, but one large open pickup truck passed us. It was piled high with melons. The driver gave us a cheerful wave as he passed. Then we saw him pull onto the side of the road and begin to back up toward us. He climbed out of his cab and stuck out his large calloused hand, "Something tells me that you fellows might enjoy eating some of my melons. Just help yourselves to as many as you would like."

We rushed to the cart and ate enough melons to qualify for the *Guinness Book of Records*. Even so, we paused to thank God and to sing "How Good Is the God We Adore."

It turned out the driver was a Christian. "When I passed you and your cart," he said, "I just knew I had to stop and give you these melons. It was as if I had orders out of a clear blue sky."

---

* I once saw a beggar woman in Madras, India, who was so emaciated that she looked as though she were starving, but she had a huge fatty tumor growing out from her side. This kind of tumor is called a lipoma and is made of millions of fat cells. Under the microscope these cells are normal in appearance and in function, but they are called a cancer because they live for themselves rather than for the body. Most of what this woman ate was taken up by her lipoma, while the rest of her body starved.

We never missed another meal. God continued to provide—even to the last day.

I was the housekeeper on our final week, and funds again were low. We were spending the weekend in Stone, Staffordshire, just six hundred miles from where we had started. We always packed up all our formal clothes in a big trunk every Sunday night and sent it on by rail on Monday to our next weekend destination. Weekends were the only time we wore them. When we arrived at Stone, our trunk was missing. The railway could not track it down, so on Sunday we all preached in short pants and open-neck shirts.

We gathered on Monday morning, ready to take our cart to the railway station and send it back to London, while we all took the train home. It was our last meeting together as a team. All of us had started the trek already supplied with rail tickets home so that we would never have to choose between food and money for a return ticket. Now, as the last housekeeper, I had to report on the accounts. After all expenses had been paid, we had just three shillings and sixpence in our purse.

The verger of the cathedral had worked extremely hard to make all arrangements for our weekend in Stone. We knew he had a sick child at home, so we all voted that we give him our last three and sixpence. After the others had gone to the railway station with the cart, I sought him out and thanked him, giving him our little gift.

He quickly returned the money, saying he had enjoyed the service he had been able to give and couldn't accept any money. So I arrived at the railway station with the three shillings and sixpence intact. I met the others who were standing round our big trunk, which had finally turned up and was now to be forwarded to London. The station master apologized for the delay and told us that he had to collect the freight for the trunk.

"How much do we have to pay?" The question was on all our minds.

"Three shillings and sixpence, gentlemen, just three shillings and sixpence." I climbed on to the train with empty pockets and a light heart. Sitting in the train as it sped toward home, I tried to put all the experiences together. I began to realize that each of the extraordinary events of that trek were examples of the way the Spirit of God works through members of the body of Christ. The farmer who knew he had to give us melons; the verger who knew he must not take our gift; all were impulses from the Holy Spirit. All were part of the day-to-day provision that allowed fourteen men to start the trek with provisions for three days and to live and march and eat for six weeks—never missing a meal—and finish the trip with exactly no money left over, not one penny.

Trek 1936 had been a learning experience for me. Living in such spiritual intimacy with so many Christian young men and sharing physical exhaustion and spiritual testing had been a character-building experience. Never again could I doubt that God intervenes in the affairs of men and that His chosen method was at the level of the spirit, as some members of His body responded to impulses from the *Head* to meet the need of the other members.

CHAPTER 13

It Tastes Better If It's Shared

Goods which are not shared are not goods.

~ FERNANDO ROJAS, *LA CELESTINA*

One eats in holiness and the table becomes an altar.

~ MARTIN BUBER

Times when there is a shortage of food—famine or wars—reveal a lot about the culture and character of a nation and its individuals. During World War II Germany's submarine blockade off the shores of Britain was very effective. Britain is far too small and crowded to grow enough food for its population. At one time it appeared that those of us living there might be starved out.

In this sort of situation wealthy and powerful individuals often buy up large quantities of essential foods and hold them in anticipation of rising prices. Great fortunes have been made this way in many countries. However, Britain was blessed with inspiring leaders at that time, and they imposed a rigid system of rationing.

Everybody grumbled about the rationing, but few really resented it because everybody was rationed. No one was exempt. True, some did better than others because they had the money to eat out more frequently. But every home and every person was judged on the same scale. The king and queen and royal family had the same ration books, as did the ministers of state. That made everybody feel good.

During this time doctors were authorized to prescribe extra milk for people who suffered from diseases where milk was considered necessary: gastritis, for example, and peptic ulcers. This was obviously a need, and not begrudged.

I was resident surgical officer of a children's hospital in London, and it was part of my job to see that sick children received extra milk if necessary. My boss was a famous surgeon who specialized in surgical reconstruction of kidneys and bladders in children. We had a four-year-old boy who had been born with severe malformations of his only functional kidney. Terry was undersized and subject to every infection that came along. The operation was long and hazardous, but he came through it well. The nursing staff loved Terry and carefully watched his diet. He liked—and needed—milk, and we could provide plenty on my prescription.

When Terry was well enough to go home, I told his parents his diet was critical; he needed plenty of milk because he was still fragile. I gave them a certificate for extra rations.

The certificate came back—disallowed! Frustrated, I dashed off a letter to the authorities telling them about Terry and his operation on his only kidney. I underscored that his need was critical. I was sure the first certificate had been misread by some bureaucrat.

But it came back—disallowed again! This time it was accompanied by a polite letter and a long list of all the conditions for which extra milk was allowed. My earlier certificates had been allowed because the patient was in post-operative status. The kidney problem was rare and not on the list. Extra milk for post-operative patients was given only for three weeks. I took the letter to my chief, Mr. Twistington Higgins, the surgeon. He was as angry as I was, and we wrote another letter to the faceless bureaucrat who was standing in the way of the health of our little patient.

Letters flew back and forth while we contrived to find milk for the patient. Our last letter threatened to appeal to our Member of Parliament and have him ask a question in the House of Commons—the ultimate recourse of the angry Britisher.

That same week, I came down with a fierce attack of influenza, which I diagnosed as meningitis (typical of a new doctor trying to diagnose himself). I had myself admitted to my old university hospital under the care of my most loved and most trusted teacher, Sir Harold Himsworth. I knew he was authorized to use the new miracle drugs that were in short supply. He smiled at my diagnosis and prescribed some special pills (he told me later they were aspirin), and I soon felt much better.

As I was recovering, Sir Harold leaned over the end of my bed and smiled as he said, "You and I have been having an interesting correspondence the last few days! I really wish I could give extra milk to your little Terry, but I'm quite ready to advise the Minister of Health when he answers your question in the House of Commons if you decide to appeal that far!" I was utterly dumbfounded. It was my own revered professor who had denied milk to my patient! I stammered something about having no idea that I was writing to him, and he told me that his replies had been signed by the bureaucrats but that he made the final decisions on difficult cases and chaired the committee that laid down the rules.

He told me he was proud of me for fighting for the case of little Terry. He agreed that Terry ought to have extra milk and was sure I was getting it for him one way or another. He cocked his head sideways in a question, and I nodded to say that indeed he was not actually going without milk.

That day I gained a rare inside look at how a bureaucracy works in setting up a rationing program. First, enormous care is taken to think up a list of all diagnoses that involve real need for milk. Then you have to recognize that many people, doctors included, are going to try to find a way around the regulations and prescribe it for cases where there is no real need. Since there is no time to follow-up individual cases, one just has to close the door to exceptions.

"You would not believe," he told me, "the stories we get. Every one is different, and they all sound worthy, but if we open the door, it would become a flood. We would have to cut the ration for everybody to keep enough for a mixed bag of need and of good storytellers.

"What usually happens in cases of real need is that local people get together and find a solution. That's good; it makes for togetherness. We would find it impossible to sort out real needs from false, but at the level of the family or the church, they know what really goes on."

He went on, "You'll be glad to know that your letters had one good effect. They made us hurry up and close a loophole we knew was there but had not bothered to close. We believe all young children need extra milk, but so far it has been given to infants until they are three and then again to all elementary school children, which starts at five years of age. Four-year-olds fall between! That has always seemed silly. Now, partly because of your letters, four-year-olds are going to have extra milk.

"So now Terry can get his milk—not because he has a weak kidney and not because of your certificate, but because he is four years old!" Sir Harold grinned like a schoolboy and moved away, still smiling.

GOD'S RATIONING SUCCESS STORY

One of the best accounts of rationing that successfully prevented starvation is recounted in Genesis 40–45. What's unique about this story is that the rationing started long before the famine. No physical miracle occurred or was called for during this success story. The evidence that God was in control of the situation was that miracles occurred at the level of the mind and the spirit. God gave Joseph wisdom in all that he did and helped him to use the resources he already had.

The story begins when Joseph was a boy, the favorite son of his father, Jacob. Jacob had had a checkered career, with many deceptions and questionable practices. However, Jacob's faith in God was genuine. He had probably told Joseph many times about his face-to-face meeting with God at Peniel and about his dream at Bethel and God's covenant with him. After growing up hearing about God's direct intervention in his father's life, Joseph was prepared to believe his own dream and vision that he would become ruler. He remembered it and viewed it as a promise from God all through his times of imprisonment and hardship.

Then God saw to it that Joseph was trained to be a good administrator. He began as a slave in Potiphar's house and was promoted to become chief administrator of a large household and business. After he was in prison, his natural ability and his integrity won the confidence of the chief jailor, and Joseph became the administrator of a whole prison, significant training for political office.

Dreams come back into the story again when Joseph won the confidence and admiration of the chief butler by interpreting a dream he had. When the butler was released from prison, he promised to plead for Joseph's release—but he forgot! If he had remembered and Joseph had been released, God's plan for providing food during the upcoming famine might not have been accomplished. As a free man Joseph would have become lost to the sequence of Pharaoh's affairs.

But in God's timing even forgetfulness can play an important role! As it turned out, at the precise moment when Pharaoh was most troubled by his dreams and upset by the incompetence of his advisors, the butler finally remembered Joseph. He was called up from prison, and Pharaoh told him his dreams. God gave Joseph the insight to interpret the dreams to Pharaoh and the impudence to go ahead and tell the ruler of all Egypt what he should do.

Even when he was in prison, Joseph knew he was somebody special in God's plans. He had a Spirit-induced self-esteem. He knew his wisdom was God's wisdom, so he wasn't afraid to confront Pharaoh.

In spite of all the hardships he encountered, Joseph never asked God to cancel the famine. He never asked for a way out. He used the resources God had provided and advised that Egypt use its years of plenty to prepare for the years of famine.

So started the greatest project of food conservation the world had ever known. We don't know how the Egyptian farmers reacted to what amounted to a huge increase in taxation on their profits. We can only imagine the grumbling. (If Pharaoh had been up for reelection after the first four of the seven years of plenty, he might have been in trouble if his opponent had promised to reduce taxes!)

We don't know what would have happened in Egypt without Joseph and his plan for rationing. During the years of surplus the Egyptian farmers probably would have used their surplus grain to become rich. The economy would have improved; the GNP would have posted gains. An extra pyramid or two might have been built. Those who warned that the good times could not last and that conservation should be practiced for the sake of the future would have been called doomsayers.

Joseph! We need you today!

As we look back on what Joseph did, it seems an obvious thing to do: use times of plenty to prepare for future times of hardship. The trouble is, hindsight isn't available when it's needed. We have to use foresight, and foresight is a rare commodity. Today, future harvests are being jeopardized by greedy demands for higher living standards. We are building up debts today that our grandchildren will have to repay in a future that will have more mouths to feed and fewer resources to draw from. Most people seem to give little thought to conserving for generations to come.

Where shall we find our Joseph for today's years of plenty?

We can begin by praying that God will prepare such a man or woman with vision and leadership and that we will recognize God's person. We need to be willing to simplify our own lifestyles and become examples of joyful living within limits that will not make it harder to provide food in the decades to come.

In the meantime, as children of God, let's learn to conserve all the good things in the earth that God intended to last and last. Let's conserve the fossil fuels. Let's take vacations nearer home. Let's ride the bus or train rather than ride alone in a car. Let's bicycle or walk to work or play. Let's redecorate our old houses rather than building new ones. These are the things all generations before us have had to do and what every generation after us will have to do when the oil and gas are used up or have become too expensive.

The good news is that more and more people are sounding the alarm, and conservation is gradually appearing on the political agenda. More individuals and families are recycling and trying to avoid waste.

MULTIPLYING YOUR RESOURCES

Up to this point we've focused on physical food and resources. At this point you might be asking, "How does this apply to my spiritual life?" When as Christians we talk about management of spiritual food, we need to focus on sharing rather than rationing.

Sharing is quite different from rationing, and different from a levy. It's voluntary and born of love and concern instead of rules and necessity. It has a special relevance to spiritual food and then spills over to the whole of life.

When you share spiritual food, it doubles. In fact, it's more than doubled. I learned this from watching Bishop Taylor Smith.

Bishop Taylor Smith, who had been chaplain general to the British armed forces in World War I, retired after that war to become a bishop-without-portfolio. He was loved by the evangelical wing of the Anglican Church and Christians of all stripes.

The bishop always awakened early in the morning and spent an hour in reading and meditation. His prayer was that God would give him a special thought during that hour, one that would stay with him all day to inspire and encourage him.

Thus equipped, Taylor Smith would sally forth to his duties, keeping his "best thought" in mind. I knew the bishop when I was in my teens, and whenever I saw him coming toward me, I knew I had to think fast. Sooner or later he would ask, "Paul, what is your best thought for today?" He didn't expect any profound or theological answer. It was enough for me to quote a Scripture or to say, "I have realized that I do not get things done any faster by worrying about them, so I am not going to get anxious today." Then the bishop would happily tell me his own "best thought" for the day.

We exchanged many best thoughts. I don't remember any of them exactly. Most were simple and down-to-earth. I do remember that after talking with Bishop Taylor Smith my thoughts were turned toward God. He helped me to keep on track, to put first things first.

I sometimes watched the bishop as he greeted others and talked with them. Each one seemed to leave with a lighter step. I couldn't help but compare what the bishop was doing with what Jesus did with the loaves and fishes. Every day the bishop was multiplying his bread by sharing it with others.

It's a principle that works every time: Whenever something is shared, it multiplies. When we share material food, it establishes some kind of bond. It enhances flavor, too. The fact that our own meal is diminished enriches the taste of what is given as well as what is left behind.

IT TASTES BETTER IF IT'S SHARED

Earlier I said that we need another Joseph. Perhaps that's not necessary. After all, the same Holy Spirit that prepared and inspired Joseph is available today. God can start a movement through His church that will change our country and the world. He can make us faithful to His vision for the future. Part of that vision will involve the kind of personal discipline of simplicity and sharing that Jesus modeled.

I've said this already, but I'll say it again: The simple life is a joyful life. The joy comes partly from sharing what God has given—whether physical or spiritual.

I remember my mother's first attempt to grow strawberries on the Kolli Hills. Six plants grew, but as a whole the crop was a failure. Only one plant grew a strawberry to eatable size, maybe a little more than an inch across. We watched it grow and protected it from birds. Finally the great day came to harvest it. We took a saucer and put a spoonful of cream in the middle. The strawberry was then placed in the cream and carefully cut lengthwise into four sections. Father, Mother, my sister, and I each took a teaspoon and ate our quarter strawberry, scooping up enough cream to get the proper mix. We chewed slowly, waiting as long as possible to swallow. It was the first strawberry I had ever tasted, and I have never enjoyed any strawberry more than that since then. It had been a ritual of fellowship.

Thirty-five years later my wife and I were having a holiday in the Nilgiri Mountains of South India with our six-year-old son and our two younger daughters. We called on the pastor of the little church up there, and he offered Christopher a big strawberry from his garden and his little sister a smaller one. Christopher asked for them both to be divided, and Mr. Merriweather commented that it was okay for him to eat the big one, since it had been given to him. The little boy looked up solemnly and said, "It'll taste better if it's shared."

Mr. Merriweather was so tickled at the profound message from a small boy that he brought it into his sermon the next Sunday, to Christopher's acute embarrassment. He told the story again a couple of Sundays later. Christopher could never understand what the fuss was about. He was only repeating a basic truth of our family life that had been passed from generation to generation.

All of life really does taste better if it is shared.

CHAPTER 14

Celebration of Self-Discipline

Corruptible flesh made not the soul to sin; the sinning soul made the flesh corruptible.

~ St. Augustine

I am not hungry; but thank goodness, I am greedy.

~ Punch magazine, 1878

Ramaswamy, my Indian patient and friend, was physically ugly. Leprosy had distorted his face and his hands so much that he was beyond surgical help for physical restoration. He was unable to make a living and had long accepted the status of a beggar. His downcast eyes and whining voice shouted to the world that he felt worthless to himself and to society.

He came to our New Life center originally to learn a trade, but his hands were so stiff and clenched that he couldn't hold tools. We were unable to help him—at least physically. However, during his stay he came to know Jesus Christ, was baptized, and took the name Paul. His whole attitude and demeanor changed completely. He started holding up his head and smiling. We discovered he was a quick learner and a good teacher. He began teaching some of the younger patients how to take care of their hands, using his own as examples of what might happen if they ignored his advice.

Groups of medical students often visited our center, wanting to learn about leprosy. Soon we had Paul teaching them the principles of rehabilitation. Many commented on the joy they saw in his face. He loved talking about Jesus.

In 1991 at the annual awards ceremony of the medical college, the principal of the college presented Paul with a certificate that honored him as the teacher of the year. Paul's body had failed him. His psyche had accepted defeat. But Jesus Christ took hold of his spirit and used it to restore and enliven his mind so that his physical limitations were insignificant. Not only was he a good teacher, the students voted him the best.

I tell you this story because it so powerfully illustrates what I, as a Christian and a physician, believe about the interdependence of the spirit, mind, and body. Healing that starts in the spirit can quickly affect the mind and from there many of the functions of the body.

TREATING THE WHOLE PERSON

Most physicians, when they consider health and sickness, think only of the roles of the body and the mind: the *soma* and the *psyche*. They practice psychosomatic medicine. Many Christians, when they consider health and sickness, speak only about the body and the spirit. They may see psychological ills as manifestations of sin—or at the least lack of faith.

Both camps have only two-thirds of the truth. The body is the palpable structure that houses the brain, the seat of the mind. It is not possible to pin down an anatomic location for the spirit, but it is central to all the rest. God is spirit, and we are created in His image. The human mind was designed to be the instrument of the spirit and to be the control center for the body. Many of the ills of the body are the result of the rebellion of our spirit against the control of the Spirit of God.

When we accept the lordship of Christ, our spirit, in harmony with its Creator, begins to remove conflict from our mind. In its new freedom, the mind is better able to control the body, until we experience that inner peace and harmony that is the foundation of true health.

We can't leave out the spirit. Some Christian doctors, myself included, say we practice pneumo-psychosomatic medicine (*pneuma* is Greek for "spirit"). We recognize the oneness and the interdependence of spirit, mind, and body.

So, if someone who is overweight comes to me for help, I consider that person's mind and spirit as well as his or her body. Obviously, eating is a function of the body. A normal, everyday sense of hunger is based on impulses from the stomach and is perceived in the mind, which initiates action in response to hunger. However, the spirit also affects the physical process of hunger and digestion and participates in control of those parts of the mind that are involved with physical hunger and appetite.

The psyche—the mind—is at the center of appetite. The mind may generate feelings of hunger even when there's no physical need. The sight of food, well prepared and nicely displayed, can stimulate the imagination enough to make one want to eat. The act of eating can stimulate feelings of well-being and elation. Sadly, this is common in people who have poor self-images and are overweight. Soon after a put-down experience, they go and eat, perhaps alleviating their psychological need but often adding to their weight problem. People who eat in response to a low self-esteem really need the help of somebody who understands pneumo-psychosomatic medicine or counseling.

In general, one may note that the mind, out of control, will tend to choose the path of immediate gratification of any natural appetite, restrained only by the prospect of short-term bad results. The Spirit introduces other priorities and helps the mind accept disciplines that have long-term benefits for the individual and for others, for the body of Christ and ultimately for the kingdom of God.

HEALING BEGINS IN THE SPIRIT

When people want to lose weight, they are usually put on strict diets. They start counting calories, eating fat-free foods, and even buying exercise machines to work out every day. A weight-loss program is effective if the problem is simply physical. But if there is a strong psychological component, one must go further.

Because of the peer pressure and competition prevalent among teenagers, many high school girls have food addictions, such as compulsive eating. A compulsive eater may keep to her diet, except for the times she feels an overwhelming compulsion to eat. She will suddenly begin eating everything in sight, as though she were trying to escape from starvation. Later, back on her diet, she may be at a loss to explain what has happened.

Psychologists may call this a compulsive neurosis, and they would be partly right. Such a neurosis may progress to a really serious mental reversal of normal appetite control, resulting in *anorexia nervosa*, in which a person may so turn against food that she starves to death.

When a spiritual counselor is consulted by someone with one of these mind-based eating disorders, he or she must find out whether there are deeper problems that are the cause of her compulsive behavior. In some cases the counselor may discover that the girl has evaluated herself beside her peers and has given herself a failing grade. This is not an academic grade; it's how she feels about herself as a person and how she feels she's regarded by her peers. If none of the boys look at her twice and if she thinks her friends laugh at her behind her back, she may feel absolutely worthless.

If so, she needs help to accept a new evaluation of herself as a person. Who is it that determines the worth of any one of us? On what basis should our worth be judged? This is a question the mind alone may find hard to answer. The evidence of the senses and of people around us may only reinforce one's sense of worthlessness. It is only when our spirit turns to God and we see ourselves as one for whom Christ died that we may begin to realize our infinite worth in His sight. A fellow member of the body of Christ is one best able to work with another member who is disturbed. We sometimes need the physical touch of a friend to reassure us that we are loved and worth something to our fellow members as well as to our Head. Once we can get across to the minds of the sufferers that they are loved *as they are*, then they may relax and begin to enjoy the discipline of making themselves even better fitted to fulfill God's will for their lives. This may include a discipline for losing weight, or it may include getting along with oneself even though one's shape remains the same.

The story of Zacchaeus offers some insights about the way Jesus brought spirit-mind wholeness where it was sorely needed. Zacchaeus was a man with a poor self-image. He was very small. Perhaps because he couldn't hold his head up among his peers, he had turned his back on his fellow citizens and gone to work for the Romans as a tax collector. He was hiding in a tree, hoping to see Jesus without being seen himself, when Jesus looked up at him and announced: "Zacchaeus, hurry and come down, because I want to stay at your house tonight!"

Suddenly Zacchaeus became a new man. Jesus was coming to his home! The great Jesus, the talk of the town, the prophet, had publicly proclaimed that he had chosen to stay at the Zacchaeus home! In one tumultuous moment, Zacchaeus knew that he was somebody. It opened the door to his heart; he repented and committed his life to the One he now called Lord.

Many people need a Zacchaeus type of revelation—a moment when they recognize that God himself has looked at them, has seen all their blemishes, and still wants to live in their home, being identified as their guest.

LEARNING TO VALUE SELF-DISCIPLINE

Let me say again that body, mind, and spirit work together. The physical body is controlled within itself by many automatic reflexes but looks to the mind for control of voluntary activity. The mind in turn looks to the spirit for guidance about living in submission to the overall strategies and priorities of life and of relationship to God. Paul expresses this relationship clearly: "Those who live according to the sinful nature have their *minds* set on what that nature desires; but those who live in accordance with the Spirit have their *minds* set on what the Spirit desires. The mind of sinful man is death, but the mind controlled by the Spirit is life and peace" (Romans 8:5–6, italics added).

Those who live according to this verse are living in submission to the will of God. This is contrary to our human nature and requires discipline, something that has become increasingly rare. There are a few places where self-discipline is still valued, as in athletics and the military, but for the most part pride in the mastery of oneself is being replaced by instant self-gratification.

Many people no longer require their children to exercise self-discipline. I believe that's one reason there are so many overweight children in America. No one has helped them develop discipline about food; they have been allowed to eat whatever they want whenever they want it.

Parents often feel it's unkind to deny their children snacks when food is available. These parents need to know how such lack of discipline affects their child physically. Early in life, the cells that store body fat multiply in response to the amount of fat that is there to store. In later years these extra fat cells may remain in the body and express their need to be fed by creating a sense of hunger. An adult who has extra fat cells will have a difficult time dieting and resisting the cravings of his or her fat cells. Those who have never overeaten don't develop those extra cells and are spared the agony of deprivation later.

Gluttony, which is a lack of self-discipline about intake of food, is an expression of pure hedonism. This philosophy advocates that pleasure is the highest good. So, if eating is pleasurable, then "eat, drink and be merry, for tomorrow we die."

During the decline of the Roman Empire, the Romans turned increasingly to hedonistic feasting and drunkenness. Their banquet tables displayed mountains of food. The Romans gorged themselves and then made room for more by reaching their fingers down their throat to stimulate vomiting. After a brief rest they returned to the tables to eat again. Hedonism certainly, but not happiness.

Gluttony leads to frustration and misery. God designed us so that eating is only pleasurable when we need to eat. The more we eat, the less we need to go on eating. If we insist on eating more, we'll feel nauseated.

If a person overeats most of the time, his digestive tract eventually turns on him. Too much of anything—too much food, too much alcohol—causes the natural rhythms of one's internal chemistry to change. Overeating begets pain, not pleasure. The only lasting heritage of the glutton is his excessive bulk. Even walking can become difficult as the joints begin to wear out from carrying too much weight for too long.

A gourmet is a person who enjoys fine food and cultivates a taste for it. If he exercises self-discipline as well and eats only when he is hungry, eating will remain enjoyable. The philosophy of "enough is enough" will actually stretch his capacity to experience pleasure.

EACH PART WORKING TOGETHER

God has created us primarily so we could have fellowship with His own Spirit, and also so we could participate in community, in the fellowship of families and of His body, the church. We can't achieve real and lasting happiness in isolation. Only in working together, eating together, and loving each other can we experience the deeper happiness God has for us.

God created the mind to be an instrument of the spirit and the body to be an instrument of the mind. Just as an athlete disciplines the body in order for it to run faster, so our bodies need to be disciplined in all their appetites and faculties, so that they are fully responsive to our will as it responds to the will of God.

I remember when Jean Benoit first won the Boston Marathon. Reporters crowded round her at the finish line, and one asked her if it had not been a terrible strain to run and keep ahead for all those miles. "No," she replied, "I was enjoying myself. My body was talking to me all the time, and I was listening to it. I know my muscles and my tendons so well that they encourage me to use them as hard as I can. They know that when they tell me to ease up a little, I will do that. I trust my body, and we enjoyed the race together."

But we can't have this kind of relationship with our bodies without discipline. Every separate sense and appetite has to learn that it is part of a greater whole. As Benoit trained her limbs to accept greater and greater stress, so they became able to run faster and enjoy it more.

As a hand surgeon, I delight in watching a good pianist playing a difficult piece of music. Harmony results from pure discipline. When someone plays the piano, each of the more than thirty muscles that control the fingers is under precise control by its own nerve cells. Every muscle is responding to the feedback from the sensory nerves in the fingertips, telling the motor nerves just when the keys have been hit with the correct force. Yet the pianist's mind is scarcely conscious of finger movement; it's concentrating on the music and enjoying it. The ability to forget the muscles and leave them to control themselves is only possible when there has been the discipline of practice every day.

In the late 1950s there was a student in the High Clerc American school in South India who was an athlete and a musician. Roger was near the end of his graduation year. A son of missionaries, he loved God and was a fine musician. He wanted to become a concert pianist. At the annual sports meet, Roger won the high jump and broke the school record in doing so. Cheers turned to cries as the school saw that he had landed outside the sand pit, on his outstretched right hand. Both bones of his lower forearm were broken and were poking out through his skin into the gravel.

The principal drove all day and night to rush Roger to our hospital. I met them in the emergency room and unwrapped the wound. The broken ends of the bones were still projecting and full of pieces of gravel and dust. I took him to the operating room, knowing that the lacerated tendons and infected bones carried the broken hopes of his career as a pianist.

I'll never forget that long operation, cleaning out dirt, cutting back the grimy bone ends, cutting off loose tags of tendons, and finally trying to put the bone ends together so they would heal properly. I dared not use screws or pins because the wound was infected. The edges of the skin had to be left open to allow the infection to drain out.

Each time I tried to hold the bones steady while my assistant began to apply a plaster cast, they would slip out of position. Finally I did something I'd never done before. I put my gloved fingertip down, between all the tendons, and rested it on the junction between the bone fragments. Then, holding it there, where I could feel exactly even the tiniest movement of the bones, I told my assistant to apply a plaster cast with my gloved finger in place.

As the plaster of Paris was applied, I was able to keep constantly in control of the bones, correcting with pressures from my left hand every movement I felt with my right index finger. We waited until the plaster cast had set, and then I wriggled my finger out of the glove. I left the glove finger in the wound and filled it loosely with sterile dressing.

Later, we removed the cast, taking out the glove, and applied a final cast. The X-ray showed the bones were in perfect alignment, but nobody could tell the extent to which the tendons and bone might adhere and prevent full finger movement. Roger left with a swollen and stiff hand, but the bones and skin had healed.

Years later I was lecturing on muscles and tendons at Chapel Hill Medical College in North Carolina. In the middle of my lecture, there was a disturbance at the door, and a message came to the platform saying there was a young man outside who said he must see me during the lecture. In walked Roger. He said he felt sure the students and doctors would like to see his hand. I told them his story while he held up his fingers, doing five finger exercises. His hand was perfect! He told us he was still a pianist. I asked him how he had gotten his fingers moving so well. He said, "Discipline, sir, that and practice." He also said that having the bones in good position must have been a help.

It takes discipline to teach every muscle in the forearm and hand just how to respond to musical notes on the score. It had taken further discipline for Roger to force himself to move his muscles against pain, as he had to stretch the fibrous bands of scar tissue every time he hit a note. But now he was master of his hand and master of music. He could delight hundreds of people at a time, translating Beethoven into liquid sound. He no longer had to think about his fingers or his tendons; that was all in the past. He had achieved inner harmony and now was free to express himself.

I used to be puzzled about why Jesus, in John 8:31–32, talks about freedom and about obedience in almost the same breath. He says that if we live in obedience to His teaching, we shall know the truth, and the truth will set us free. Free from what? The need to obey? I don't think so. We have only to turn back to Jesus' own words in John 7:16 where He says that He himself does not speak His own words but only what His Father tells Him to say. I believe that Jesus was saying that when we obey His teaching, we will be free to do what we really want to do. In other words, spiritual discipline brings spiritual freedom.

Roger really wanted to be able to play the piano, but his mind and his muscles were not in harmony. So he entered into a training period of discipline for his hand. He wanted his fingers to be true disciples of his head. Through discipline, he overcame his stiffness, and his fingers and brain became completely coordinated. His fingers had become a true extension of his mind. Everything worked together in harmony.

God's plan for the human body—and for His body, the church—is that all members would desire the same things that are wanted by the Head. When we all want the same things, the body is joyful—and it is free. We are designed to want what is good. Obedience to God helps us to know ourselves and master ourselves, just as Roger mastered his hands. Their freedom was an extension of his joy and could also bring happiness to a whole concert hall full of listeners.

FASTING AS SELF-MASTERY

When we fast we are disciplining our body's intake of food. It demonstrates that our stomach is an instrument, a servant, and can be trained to go without food for a day, even a week, without harm. When practiced within reasonable physical limits, fasting benefits the body by using up excessive stored fat while preserving the best of its tissues. There have been recent reports that fasting may even be helpful in the control of certain cancers. The rapidly growing and multiplying cancer cells apparently suffer more from lack of food than normal cells do.

When I was in the missionary training colony, we fasted occasionally as a discipline of prayer and to prove to ourselves that we could handle going without food if ever we had no food.

This self-discipline helped prepare us for rough conditions in the future. Such discipline brings a wonderful sense of self-mastery as the body is becoming used to obedience and servanthood. When guided by the Spirit, it also brings God pleasure.

A FAST UNTO DEATH

An outstanding event occurred in the mountains of South India, where I grew up. The local church was made up of members who had come to know the Lord through my father's and mother's witness. When problems arose, the whole group would meet together for discussions and for prayer. At times of real stress and challenge, my father would call for a period of prayer and fasting. This was no surprise to Indian people, who have great respect for any person who accepts personal deprivation on behalf of a community.

You might recall the old caricature of an Indian fakir lying on a bed of nails. This isn't a farfetched image. India has a strong tradition of so-called "holy men" who inflict harsh disciplines on themselves and are respected for their willingness to do so.

One day the church leaders discovered that a serious offense had been committed and that it must have involved a member of the church. I never knew just what it was, but I suspect someone had embezzled church funds. Nobody confessed, and my father felt sure that more than one person knew about it and that it pointed to a serious failure of loyalty and community.

Meetings for prayer and fasting were called, and there was much soul searching but no clues for solving the mystery. Finally my father called the little church together and spoke solemnly about the meaning of unity and how hidden sin could destroy it. Then he made his announcement. He, personally, would begin to fast and would keep it up until the sin was confessed and the mystery solved. In effect he was beginning a fast that might end in death.

This was a real bombshell. Nobody doubted father meant it. Our family found it difficult to believe that Papa really might die in his effort to restore integrity to the church. We ate meals without him, but food had lost its appeal. There were many comings and goings as senior church members came to our little wooden bungalow to plead with him to take some food. Groups of members could be seen talking earnestly together. One day passed and then another and another, and Mother's strained cheerfulness was wearing thin. We children cried as we prayed at night.

Then it broke. A group of men came into Papa's office and told him they wanted to confess. The door was closed, and we could only imagine what was said. There was prayer, and there were tears. At last Papa came out and squeezed an orange and drank the juice. He joined us at the next meal. He had ended his fast.

That fast helped me to understand the mission of Jesus on earth. The people of Israel had always looked upon God as high and powerful and holy. They associated Him with the idea of support when they were good and punishment when they sinned. They feared Him, but perhaps there was not much love in that fear. Then Jesus came. He came to suffer with them and for them, for their sin, not His. His first action after His public baptism was to fast for forty days. In the succeeding months He accepted physical and spiritual discipline of all types, all on behalf of His sinful people.

My father's fast transformed his relationship with the people. He was no longer the great foreign teacher and preacher; he had become their own dear pastor who was willing to die in order to help them to grow spiritually. By being willing to suffer, he identified himself with the people whose fault it was. His fasting said, more powerfully than words, that in the body of Christ, when one member suffers, all must suffer together.

Twenty-five years later, Mahatma Gandhi was using the instrument of his own "fast unto death" to mobilize the devotion of millions of Indians and to bring pressure on the British government to grant independence to his country. Although he never became a Christian, Gandhi always acknowledged that it was the life of Jesus that taught him the principle of suffering on behalf of others.

God has given us all things richly to enjoy, and He expects us to enjoy the act of eating. I believe the enjoyment is enhanced if we make a point of expressing gratitude and also if we use both our times of eating and our times of abstinence as opportunities for growth.*

---

* For those who would like to explore the subject of personal discipline further, I do recommend a fine book titled *Celebration of Discipline* by Richard Foster.

CHAPTER 15

A Little Leaven

The night is mother of the day
The winter of the spring,
And even upon old decay,
The greenest mosses cling.

~ JOHN GREENLEAF WHITTIER, A DREAM OF SUMMER

Have you never heard the saying, "A little leaven
leavens all the dough"? The old leaven of corruption
is working among you. Purge it out, and then you will
be bread of a new baking.

1 CORINTHIANS 5:6–7 NEB

People living in Bible times had no freezers or refrigerators, and their food had no chemical preservatives. Housewives had to constantly be on guard for food spoilage. They ate food while it was fresh or soon after it had been cooked.

Even today, in less-developed countries, the loss of food by spoilage is high. In India we were told that the best way to help feed the masses would be to help people prevent the spoilage of food they already had. This included provision of rat-and-insect-proof storage bins where food could be kept safe and dry and, if possible, cool.

The great Louis Pasteur first helped the world to understand that fermentation and corruption in food and wine was not due simply to the process of the aging of food but was the active work of microscopic living creatures. Yeasts and fungi and bacteria, falling into food or blown there by the wind, were able to break it down and use the energy of the food to promote their own growth and multiplication. In so doing they changed the nature of the food. Sometimes the changes were appreciated, as when yeasts changed sugar into alcohol and released bubbles of simple gases such as carbon dioxide, turning grape juice into wine.

In other cases the food was broken down into unpleasant or toxic substances that gave rise to bad smells, thus warning prospective eaters not to eat what had "gone bad." Still more dangerous are bacteria such as botulinus, which grows without producing any change in taste or smell but produces a toxin that results in paralysis when eaten.

Those of us who live in industrial countries should be grateful that most food has a long shelf life—we enjoy food long after it has been harvested and prepared. But we need to be careful about the preservatives that make this possible. Even though the quantities are carefully regulated most of the time, a preservative—any preservative—is effective only because it kills living organisms that would otherwise cause decay. Thus if we eat a lot of food that contains preservatives, we accumulate a lot of chemicals that are anti-life.

I eat fresh food as much as possible. I like to see holes and blemishes in the fruit and vegetables I buy because I feel that if a caterpillar took a couple of bites and survived, that is pretty good proof that the fruit carries no chemicals that might harm me.

When I picked fruit as a child, the orchards were always buzzing with wasps and fruit flies. We tried to pick the plums that a wasp was just starting to eat—that way we knew it was ripe. Today's commercial orchards have no sign of life. No birds; no bees. I know, on general principles, that what poisons wasps would also kill me if I ate enough of it. I just hope that whoever sprayed poison on those fruit trees thought about his kids and mine, at least as much as he thought about his margin of profits!

Bible writers didn't know that bacteria and yeasts were living organisms, but they did know what happened to grape juice and food when left uncooked. They found ways to use some of the changes to their advantage. Women in Israel would each keep their own culture of yeast going year after year. Even through the wanderings in the wilderness, each family carried its own kneading trough, and every few days they would knead fresh dough in the trough and bake fresh bread.

They never used all the dough they had made. They kept a little after the dough had risen, to preserve the culture of the yeast. Keeping that small amount of dough allowed the yeast to go on multiplying until it was highly concentrated. A few days later fresh dough was added to the kneading trough and kneaded with the old yeast until it was distributed throughout the dough. In the warm climate, the yeast multiplied fast in the fresh dough, and the bubbles of gas made the dough rise. Month after month the same yeast made hundreds of loaves of bread.

That's the good side of yeast. It has a bad side, too. Yeast is alive, and it can get out of hand. When it gets into other food, it quickly starts fermentation and spreads to cause corruption. People whose general state of health is low may even have yeast infect their throats and spread into other parts of the body, just like other bad germs.

The Israelites knew about the bad side of yeast and were careful to keep it away from any food they wanted to preserve. They recognized there was a living influence, similar to decay, that spread through the whole mass. When offerings of food were sacrificed to God, they always had to be without yeast. They called it leaven, and bread that was offered to God always had to be unleavened.

They were allowed to use leavened bread in peace offerings and wave offerings because these were celebrations of their own first fruits and harvest rather than burnt offerings to God. Fermented honey was never offered to God; it carried an aura of decay. Israelites could drink it at home, but they were considered imperfect.

Passover, the feast that celebrates the greatest event in Israel's history, is a special occasion for having unleavened bread. The original Passover had been an occasion for haste, so the memorial Passover feast was eaten in a hurry. Every Israelite had to be dressed for flight. The people stood around the table with sandals on and walking sticks in their hands. They ate roast lamb whose blood had been sprinkled around the doorposts and lintel, and they ate bread that had been quickly prepared by mixing fresh wheat flour and water and salt, baked immediately and without yeast.

In the celebration of the Passover, year after year, the Israelites followed the tradition of unleavened bread as well as the tradition of eating it in a hurry and in their traveling clothes, even if they had nowhere to go and nothing else to do that day. They were reliving a high moment of history: the escape from slavery in Egypt.

When Jesus and the disciples ate the Lord's Supper, they were celebrating the Passover. No doubt the bread Jesus blessed and broke and passed around at the communion supper was unleavened.

I must confess to a sneaking wish that we nonconformist Christians still used unleavened bread at our communion service. I don't mean the little round wafers that, though unleavened, are nothing like the bread that the Jews used and use today. Unleavened bread is a staple of diet in parts of India. "Chapatis" are simply made of stone-ground wheat flour mixed into stiff dough with water and salt. The dough is patted back and forth between the hands, and then, with a final flourish, it is slapped firmly onto the underside of the sloping wall of an open-topped conical earthenware that has charcoal on its floor. Held there by its moisture, it falls into the charcoal when it is cooked. The process of making, slapping, and final retrieval of the chapati from the oven is a highly skilled operation. With becoming modesty I claim to have become an expert in the art. I would be happy to bake this Indian bread at our church for communion as unleavened bread if they were to ask me.

Since yeast was recognized as a symbol of corruption and decay down through the ages and as such was forbidden from any sacrifice to God, it seems to me that unleavened bread should be used in communion services as the symbol for the body of Christ. Jesus was the only human who lived an uncorrupted life. Even in death, His body never saw corruption. He was a perfect sacrifice to God. He is our Passover, and we partake of His virtue as we identify ourselves with His sacrifice of himself.

Of course there's nothing in the Bible that says yeast itself is evil and shouldn't be eaten. It's part of God's creation and is part of the system whereby all living things are recycled. Their complex molecules are broken down to form the simple building blocks of which new living creatures can be made and by which they can be nourished. It's really a beautiful system, and I believe we should help our children understand and appreciate it.

When our children were young, we had a lot of animals as pets. We had dogs, cats, mice—even a dear skunk called

Simon. With that kind of household, death in the family was inevitable. When a pet died we would bury its body and plant a young tree in the same hole we had dug. There's no better way to encourage prolific growth of a tree than to have a rich source of nitrogen and calcium and carbon right there among the growing roots of the tree. As the young tree grew and flowered, we would remind each other that the substance of our dear pet was now taking part in a different kind of life.

I remember a jacaranda tree in Kotagiri in the mountains, bearing beautiful flowers, probably even today. It was planted over the grave of our dearest dachshund, Winston, after he had fought against a viper that threatened our children. I think every one of us was crying as we laid that little black body in the grave and planted the jacaranda sapling over his courageous little person. On our return to Kotagiri in the following years, there was a happy rush to see how the jacaranda Winston was getting on. Even today I think our grown-up children remember Winston's tree as an example of the way the corruption of one form of life encourages prolific growth of another.

SPIRITUAL LEAVEN

Yeast or leaven is spoken of in the Bible as a symbol of how a little idea or a little false teaching can spread through a whole community. Jesus also once spoke of leaven as a symbol of how the kingdom of God would spread.

In India the easiest way to obtain yeast for our bread-making was to use the toddy, or fermented drink, that the local tribespeople used for getting drunk. My parents found themselves in a dilemma when they said people should not drink toddy, yet we used it for making our bread. We also found that the yeast from the toddy was the best local source for vitamin B. Even today I eat a little yeast extract every day to make sure I'm not short of vitamin B.

Nothing is evil of itself; it is evil if it is used in a way that causes harm. My father used the toddy as an object lesson to the Indian people. He showed how the palm juice became fermented and told them that it was yeast that turned it into toddy. Then he told them that the act of drinking the alcohol made it bad because it made them lose control and hurt each other. But the alcohol was good in the dispensary, where it was used to help keep things pure and sterile. The yeast was good in bread, and it was good for nutrition, but it became bad if it was allowed to get into food and corrupt it or produce alcohol for getting drunk.

The idols the tribespeople worshiped were made of stone and wood, which are good. Stone carvings also can be good and beautiful, but when we bow down and worship them, they become instruments of wickedness. You see, the evil is in us, not in the idol. Paul makes this clear in 1 Corinthians 8:4 when he explains why he avoids eating food that has been offered to idols. The idol itself is nothing to him, but he's doing wrong if by his actions he offends somebody to whom it does mean something.

How easily an idea spreads and gathers followers! "A little leaven leaveneth the whole lump." Let us watch out in case some exciting new idea—even a good one—takes over and turns evil because it becomes an idol in our lives, usurping the place reserved for our Lord.

When the perishable has been clothed with the imperishable, and the mortal with immortality, then the saying that is written will come true: "Death has been swallowed up in victory."

"Where, O death, is your victory?
Where, O death, is your sting?"

The sting of death is sin, and the power of sin is the law. But thanks be to God! He gives us the victory through our Lord Jesus Christ. (1 Corinthians 15:54–57)

CHAPTER 16

The Lord's Supper:
The Bread

Is not the cup of thanksgiving for which we give
thanks a participation in the blood of Christ? And
is not the bread that we break a participation in the
body of Christ?

1 CORINTHIANS 10:16

God, in a wonderful way, has demonstrated that there is
no real break in the continuum of spirit and flesh. The
fleshly act of eating and the spiritual act of worship may be
one. The nourishment of our bodies and the enrichment of our
souls may all be part of the way our life should be seen—not as
a spiritual life using a physical life as a dwelling, but intimately
one life. The Lord's Supper is a continuing feast that symbolizes the oneness of each of us with our Lord and through Him
with each other.

The Lord's Supper is the continuing center of the Christian
faith. Jesus Christ chose it as the way for the members of His
church to keep reminding themselves of all that He has done
and all that He continues to do for us. We come to the Lord's
Supper to renew our sense of oneness with our Savior and with
each other.

Jesus chose bread and wine to serve as a focus for our senses while our minds rise to spiritual realities. He told us to build a feast around the act of eating and drinking them. He even gave a spiritual content to the substance of the food and drink in that feast, saying that it was His own broken body and His blood, shed for us.

Bread symbolizes all food—it is the staff of life. When what we need to sustain life is reduced to its ultimate simplicity, it comes down to bread and water.

CHEAP BREAD OR COSTLY DISCIPLINE?

I don't know when Jesus fully recognized the nature of His mission—certainly not in His childhood. When His parents found Him in the temple, questioning the scribes, He told them, "Did you not know that I must be about My Father's business?" (Luke 2:49 NKJV). His Father's business for that period of Jesus' life was for Him to go to school and get to know the Law and the Prophets.

As He grew up Jesus must have realized more and more the nature of His relationship to God the Father and something of His mission to reveal the love of God to the people of Israel. I, personally, believe that He came to full realization of this when He was baptized. The Spirit descended on Him like a dove, and He was filled with the Spirit.

When John the Baptist pointed to Him and said, "Look, the Lamb of God, who takes away the sin of the world!" I can imagine Jesus shuddering. Every Jew knew how a lamb took away sin—it was killed and sacrificed on an altar.

Immediately after His baptism, Jesus was led by the Spirit to go into the desert, where He was tempted by the devil. This was no chance meeting; He went to the desert expressly for that meeting. Why? To face those specific temptations, as soon as He had come to realize the full physical impact of the plan of salvation and of His part in it.

Each of the three temptations Jesus experienced were really Satan's suggestions that there might be an easier way. The first was that He need not be really poor and hungry. After all, He had the power to turn stones into food. The second was to use spectacular miracles to convince the people that He was God; then He would never have to experience rejection. The last was to use worldly methods to win the world to His side. All three implied that by some form of special miracle, by the use of the special resources of the power of God or the devil, His task might be made easier.

The first temptation—"tell this stone to become bread"— helps us understand the bread of the Lord's Supper. Jesus had fasted for forty days. His hunger was real. By that time probably everything He saw looked like food, and every mirage in the desert looked like water. The ground was strewn with what looked like loaves of bread. All He had to do was to speak the word and stoop down and pick them up.

The words of the tempter were translated through Jesus' appetites.* They came disguised as a reasonable solution to a physical discomfort or to a strong desire. It took His spiritual insight to see the shadow of Satan behind His own hunger. Jesus recognized that, even though there were no witnesses, He must not break His self-imposed discipline to live as a human being with no special advantages. He had the life of the Spirit within Him, but that advantage He later shared with His body, the church.

---

* Temptation would be so much easier to resist if we could see the devil, looking like a devil, and hear him speak. I expect that Jesus was tempted in the same way that I am.

STONES INTO BREAD

Stones do become bread. It happens all the time. We call it a miracle if it happens in a moment, but all bread is a miracle. We have looked at this process before. Ancient rocks and stones have been eroded, over thousands of years, as a result of frost and heat, rain and shine. Birds drop seeds into cracks of a rock, and the growing plants deepen the cracks, splitting rocks into smaller stones. Lichens soften the surface of stones, and the dust of erosion becomes soil. The dusty soil becomes enriched by dying leaves and living worms, until it is ready for a farmer to plant a germ of wheat.

Alternating rain and sun and the farmer's care allow the growth. When heavy ears of wheat begin to bend the stalk, harvest begins, and sheaves of grain are taken to the threshing floor to be beaten by the flail or trampled by the oxen.

The grain is swept up from the floor, and when there is a modest breeze, it is winnowed free of chaff. The millstone grinds it into flour. The baker's kneading forms it into a shape, not unlike a stone, and prepares it for the oven. There in fiery heat the dough becomes a loaf of bread. If it were then placed among stones in the wilderness, the loaf might be mistaken for just another stone. It might look like its own ancestor stone, the stone that formed the soil from which its substance grew.

The miracle in that story happens when the kernel of wheat falls into the ground and seems to die. All of its visible substance dies, but the microscopic germ of life is released by the death of its visible body, and that life takes hold of the good soil, born of rocks and stones, and turns it into living growth and loaves of bread.

Jesus looked at the stones in the wilderness and made His choice. The cheap miracle that would have turned the stones directly into bread would save Him from hunger now. More than that, it would begin to bypass the whole sequence of discipline to which He had dedicated His life. I am sure Jesus already knew that He would call himself "the bread of life" and that real broken bread would later form, for His followers, the symbol of His sacrificial life and death. That bread would have passed through every stage of dying seed, then growth, threshing, grinding, kneading, and firing in the oven. Then it would be broken and shared.

If Jesus chose cheap bread, it would start Him on a pathway that would save Him from hardship and poverty for the rest of His life on earth. But instead of responding to His hunger and eating a selfish meal alone in the desert, He chose to wait and prepare a feast that would be open to all. He chose to make bread in the costly way, by which His bodily death would release for all mankind the new kind of life that would go on to eternity.

Later, when Jesus did say, "I am the bread of life. He who comes to me will never go hungry," he spoke with the memory of His own hunger and with the confidence that His flesh was real bread, made the costly way.

How much preparation it takes, much of it unseen, before a loaf of bread can appear on the table! Once there, our attention turns from how it was produced to what it means to each of us as we eat.

ONE LOAF, ONE BODY

In every human civilization, eating has become a ritual of togetherness. Families come together for food. Friends may drop in to visit, but after a few minutes, they will be offered a snack or invited to stay for a meal.

The ultimate test of a culture is the way a stranger is treated. Jesus gives commendation to those who welcome others: "I was hungry and you gave me something to eat . . . I was a stranger and you invited me in . . ."

Just as eating together is a sign of fellowship, so the refusal to eat together has been recognized as a sign of enmity or pride. One of the extraordinary sidelights that come from the story of Joseph is that even when he became ruler of all Egypt, he was not allowed to eat with the Egyptians. They certainly appreciated Joseph but had a deep-seated hatred of Hebrews. This was possibly because they despised shepherds, and Hebrews were shepherds. So the prohibition against eating with Hebrews was the visible symbol of an Egyptian inner attitude of contempt.

In the first-century church, we read repeatedly that Christians met together in one another's homes for "breaking of bread" and for "prayer." It seems that this referred both to the actual communion service of bread and wine and also to a kind of fellowship meal. Bread was often used as a symbol of food in general. Just by sharing a meal together, these early Christians were demonstrating their common life and their love for one another.

Some of the most solemn warnings ever given in Scripture in reference to the communion service were given by the apostle Paul to the church in Corinth. I believe that chapters 10 through 13 of 1 Corinthians were all intended as a rebuke to the church for its failure in the matter of fellowship, especially at the service of "breaking of bread." Included in these chapters is an inspiring outline of a better way.

It begins when Paul talks about the bread. He says, "Is not the bread that we break a participation in the body of Christ? Because there is one loaf, we, who are many, are one body, for we all partake of the one loaf" (1 Corinthians 10:16–17).

Then, in the next chapter, Paul becomes explicit in his rebuke: "I hear that when you come together as a church, there are divisions among you . . . It is not the Lord's Supper you eat, for as you eat, each of you goes ahead without waiting for anybody else. One remains hungry, another gets drunk . . . Do you despise the church of God and humiliate those who have nothing?" (1 Corinthians 11:18–22).

Then Paul goes on to speak of the need for each of us to examine himself before he partakes of the Lord's Supper, because if he is not "recognizing the body of the Lord [he] eats and drinks judgment on himself" (1 Corinthians 11:29). Now I know that the primary meaning of the phrase "recognizing the body of the Lord" must refer to the sacrificed body of Jesus Christ. However, in the context of this whole passage, it's clear that Paul intended to tell the Corinthian church that they had been failing to recognize the body of Christ right there in Corinth, sitting around them, their own fellow members of the body of Christ. He concludes this rebuke by saying, "When you come together to eat, wait for each other." In other words, don't break bread until all the loaf is prepared to celebrate its oneness together.

There is an Arabic Baptist church in Israel that has a lovely way to celebrate the breaking of bread. When they come together, each member brings a handful of grains of wheat. It may be from one's own field or from personal supplies at home. As members enter the church, they each pour their grains into a common pot. When all have come and while the worship goes on, the pot is taken to the kitchen and somebody quickly grinds the wheat in a stone mill, mixes in water and salt, and kneads the flour into a loaf. It is put into the already-heated oven and baked.

By the time the service is finished and the church moves into the celebration of the Lord's Supper and the breaking of bread, the loaf is ready. As members break off their own portions, each individual is sharing grains of flour from every member of the church. When asked why they do this, one member replied, "As individual seeds we are each alone and separate from each other. Only when we are broken into flour and baked together can we experience full fellowship."

Paul goes on to give the fullest account in Scripture of the symbolism of membership in the body of Christ (1 Corinthians 12). He is obviously continuing the theme of the oneness of the members of the body. He talks about the gifts of the Spirit and how each relates to the body as a whole. He ends the chapter by advising each of us to "eagerly desire" the best gifts. The King James Version reads, "Covet earnestly the best gifts."

I personally think that Paul looked at what he had just written and thought it might be misunderstood. (Or perhaps the Holy Spirit tapped him on the shoulder and said, "Watch it, Paul! Those Corinthians may think you are saying that people with the 'best gifts' should be honored above the rest, and they'll have a hierarchy again!") So Paul quickly adds, "And now I will show you the most excellent way." Thus begins one of the best-known chapters in the Bible, the chapter that exalts love above all gifts and says that even the highest gifts are absolutely nothing without love. That love chapter is in direct continuity with the concept that we are one loaf.

What a wonderful feast Jesus left for us to continue in remembrance of Him! What a shame the interpretation of the details of its meaning has separated Christians all over the world into their sects and perpetuated divisions among us.

I have worked and worshiped in many countries of the world and have sometimes felt lonely because I don't speak the local language and don't know any individuals at a personal level. In such situations it is a special joy to meet together with Christians and break bread together. I remember one time when I had to teach a course on leprosy rehabilitation in the University of Ankara in Turkey. I speak no Turkish, I knew nobody, and I was put up in a little hotel room for the two weeks of the course, which was by translation. The country is strongly Muslim, and I couldn't find an English-speaking Christian church.

I called the American Embassy, and they told me of an old Catholic church in the Italian Embassy, near my hotel, which hosted a simple ecumenical communion service in English and French on Sunday, after the regular Mass. There were not more than fifty of us there, and we were of diverse ethnic backgrounds. I didn't even know from what kind of church the pastor conducting the service came. All I know is that we broke bread together, on our knees, and the name of Jesus Christ was honored. We hugged each other afterwards and felt at home. The atmosphere of love and fellowship stayed with me all day.

The caste system in India is pervasive. It is changing now in many ways because India is a democracy, and the lower castes are numerically by far the largest. Thus the elected members of the legislative bodies are often low caste, and they pass laws that reserve special opportunities for the oppressed segments of society. The railways don't recognize caste, nor do the buses or most of the shops. However, in social life the barriers are still rigid, and the outcasts, though no longer called untouchables, always step aside so that high caste people can avoid the need to brush up against them. Beggars by the roadside have a peculiar whining cry, and they don't make eye contact with those who pass by.

The lowest stratum of society is the deformed leprosy patient. Doctors, lawyers, and priests are looked upon as the highest stratum and are treated with great deference. I have often been embarrassed by the way patients will bow to the ground and touch my feet before I have a chance to stop them.

In our leprosy sanitarium at Karigiri in South India we have a lovely chapel, made from stones that have been hewn from the surrounding rocky hills. In that chapel during the season of Lent, we have an early morning communion service every Wednesday. It is open to Christian staff and patients and is led by one of the doctors, who is also an ordained presbyter of the Church of South India. The numbers are few at that early hour, and we stand in a circle around the table, passing the bread and the wine from hand to hand. In turn, we speak the name of the person to our left and use the scriptural words that define the elements that we share.

On the day I remember best, the person to my right was a leprosy patient, Manikam, a beggar on whose deformed hands I had operated a few weeks before. He had come to know the Lord and was happy both in the improvement in his hands as well as in his new faith. In the hospital ward, however, it was still difficult to get him to look at the doctors as he responded to our questions. His downcast eyes still identified him as an outcast.

As the plate with the bread came around the circle, Manikam took his piece and then took the plate to pass it to me. Because his hands were still stiff from the recent surgery and plaster cast as well as from the effect of his previous disease and injuries, he fumbled and almost dropped the plate. I reached out to steady it for him. Then he turned to me and held out the bread. His back was straight, his voice was clear and strong, and his eyes looked directly into mine. "Paul," he said, "this is the body of Christ, broken for you." As I took the bread my eyes misted over, and I could hardly control my voice as I turned to pass the bread to the person on my left.

I cannot describe the delight I felt as I looked into Manikam's face and recognized the life of Jesus as he spoke the words, "The body of Christ, broken for you." It was as though my eyes had been opened and I saw a new person. Jesus had broken hands, Jesus knew pain and rejection, and it was Jesus whose life and death had brought about the sense of love and fellowship that I experienced with my patient at that time. We were one loaf, one body, and shared one Lord.

This was a miracle. Anywhere but in that situation and anytime in the past, he would have called me Doctor Brand in a humble voice, with downcast eyes. To hear my name, Paul, ring out in the chapel, with the freedom and confidence of an equal member of the same body, was a most moving thing. All of us must have felt the transformation. We thanked God for the reality behind the symbol of the broken bread, broken from the one loaf.

DISTINCTLY GOD, DISTINCTLY ME

In the sixth chapter of John, Jesus identifies himself as bread. The whole chapter is an insight both into the nature of the sacrifice of Jesus and into the meaning of the communion service that Jesus introduced later.

It started after Jesus had fed the five thousand by multiplying the loaves and fishes. When the crowds had left and Jesus crossed over the lake, quite a crowd ran around the end of the lake and found Jesus on the other side. He was not fooled into thinking they were looking for more spiritual food. They were eager to see another miracle, and they wanted another free meal. They tried a broad hint, "Our forefathers ate the manna in the desert; as it is written: 'He gave them bread from heaven to eat . . .'"

"Jesus said . . . 'It is not Moses who has given you the bread from heaven, but it is my Father who gives you the true bread from heaven. . . . I am the living bread. If anyone eats of this bread, he will live forever'" (John 6:31–32, 51).

Several times in this chapter, Jesus refers to himself as bread. First in verses 35 and 48, Jesus calls himself "the bread of life." Then, in verse 51, He says, "I am the living bread." In that connection Jesus emphasized our need to have Him abiding in us. I am not sure how significant the difference is between "living bread" and "bread of life." To me, the bread of life is something I eat to sustain my life, to keep me alive. The living bread is that which comes into me and lives on in me with its own life. This exposes us to the mystery of God in us.

This is the wonder whereby the Spirit of God may live in me as distinctly God in distinctly me. Yet, as I live my human life in the flesh, I am strengthened and energized by the food I have taken in and that has become part of my own metabolism. Both concepts can coexist, and both may be symbolized as we break bread together.

It is clear from Jesus' own words and also from the practice of the early church that the service of "breaking bread together" is intended to be at the center of our worship and fellowship. It certainly is that for me. I try to ensure that I get the full meaning of what God intends for me every time, so I have a personal discipline of remembrance every time.

When I take the bread, I try to be thankful for three aspects of that broken bread that have significance for me. First, I remember the sacrifice of Jesus on the cross, when His body was broken for me. Then I think of the way in which His life continues to sustain me today—His body, the living bread.

Then, I look around me and recognize those who are worshiping with me. I need to remind myself of our essential oneness, and I do it individually. Deliberately downplaying our differences, I seek to see Jesus in each one of them. That way it becomes indeed a love feast as well as a memorial service and, not least, a celebration of the continuing life of the Lord within me.

CHAPTER 17

The Lord's Supper: The Wine

"Whoever eats my flesh and drinks my blood has eternal life . . . for my flesh is real food and my blood is real drink."

JOHN 6:54–55

D rink from it, all of you this is my blood" (Matthew 26:27–28). This may be the most shocking statement that Jesus ever made. When He spoke similar words in John 6:54–55, it probably turned away more followers than anything else He said or did. The idea of drinking human blood was not only shocking, it was also seen as a pagan idea that would be most offensive to the most orthodox and spiritual Jews. Even His own disciples were taken aback and needed help to understand why Jesus said these things. I find the words a bit difficult to read myself.

So why did Jesus say those words? Since Jesus knew how it would sound to Jews and how they would react, He must have had a good and important lesson to teach by using those words.

Jews who knew their Scriptures would remember the laws God gave Noah as He was beginning to reestablish the human race after the flood. Since Noah was the father of the remaining human race, and these laws were given much earlier than Mosaic law, they were seen as basic for all people, not just for Jews.

God gave Noah permission to eat the flesh of animals for food but told him no one was to eat flesh that still had blood in it. Blood represented life, and people must not take blood in their food. This prohibition was later reinforced and amplified in the Law of Moses for the children of Israel:

> Any Israelite or any alien living among them who eats any blood—I will set my face against that person who eats blood and will cut him off from his people. For the life of a creature is in the blood, and I have given it to you to make atonement for yourselves on the altar; it is the blood that makes atonement for one's life. Therefore I say to the Israelites, "None of you may eat blood, nor may an alien living among you eat blood." (Leviticus 17:10–12)

The priests and Levites who offered sacrifices were allowed to eat the meat of the sacrifices (except for the whole burnt offering) as a part of their means of support. But in every case it clearly required that the meat was to be offered on the altar, and the blood was either sprinkled around or poured out at the base of the altar.

Even today, when much of the Mosaic law is ignored, most Jews eat only kosher food and buy meat only at kosher markets. As soon as any animal is slaughtered for a kosher market, all of the blood is thoroughly drained out so that no blood will be eaten. When Gentiles first had the gospel preached to them and started joining the Christian church, there was a big controversy about the extent to which Gentile Christians should be required to keep the Law of Moses. The final conclusion of the apostles and Christian council at Jerusalem was that only four items of the lengthy and complex Law of Moses should be insisted upon for Gentile believers. One concerned sex outside marriage, another prohibited eating food that had been offered to idols, and both the other two were against eating blood (eating things strangled and simply eating blood). From this we see that even to Jews who had become Christians, the idea of eating or drinking blood was not only repugnant, but totally contrary to their faith.

So why would Jesus say something that He knew would offend all the Jews? If He had been trying to tell the people that He had come to be the final sacrifice for sin, He could have said that they should eat His flesh and pour out or sprinkle His blood. The Jews would have understood it at once. They would have remembered the Passover, when a lamb was killed for each household. Its flesh was eaten at the Passover meal, and its blood was sprinkled over the doorposts and lintel, to be seen by the destroying angel, who would then pass over the house without killing anyone.

This ritual was practiced every year at the Passover feast in memory of the great salvation that God accomplished for the Jewish people. When John the Baptist saw Jesus and said, "Look, the Lamb of God, who takes away the sin of the world!" His hearers knew at once what He meant. When Jesus chose the Passover feast to announce His coming sacrifice, the disciples would have understood if Jesus had passed the bread around and said that it was His body, broken for them, and they should eat it. Then, if He had taken a pitcher of wine and poured it out or sprinkled it around, there would have been a deep sigh of understanding—and of sorrow.

Why didn't Jesus do it this way? Why did He insist on saying "drink my blood," only to see good people turn away, shaking their heads?

A SPIRITUAL TRANSFUSION

I have sometimes wondered why it was that the eating of blood was so strongly prohibited in Scripture.

Many of the prohibitions about food in the Law of Moses related to matters of hygiene and health. For example, pigs are prone to pick up a parasite that makes little cysts in muscles. When pork is not properly cooked, humans who eat it may develop a parasitic disease that is difficult to treat and that would have been incurable in Moses' time. Pig meat is safe if it is cooked thoroughly. But in the desert, and with scarce fire-wood, I am sure cooking was often skimped and that God took pork off the menu for the Israelites for health reasons. The same was true for other foods that were pronounced unclean.

But blood is not unclean in that sense. The Masai tribe in Africa regularly uses blood as part of their diet and is a strong and healthy race.

God said that blood must not be eaten because it is life. The same idea is expressed in the Law of Moses we have just referred to. Pagan tribes have the same symbolism, but they often take the opposite view. They say that since the life is in the blood, they will eat the blood of a tiger so that they may become strong and fierce or the blood of a pregnant sheep in order to become fertile.

These ideas were familiar to the Jews, and they knew that blood was symbolic of life, and of the kind of life from which the blood was taken.

In the Law, God established that "the life of a creature is in the blood . . . Therefore, I say to the Israelites, 'None of you may eat blood'" (Leviticus 17:11–12). But Jesus was not say-ing, in effect, "My life is in my blood; therefore, drink it." The unique thing about the blood of Jesus is not only that it was shed for us in sacrifice but that the quality and virtue of that life is to be shared with us. When we drink the wine in the service of the Lord's Supper, we are doing it in remembrance of the death of Jesus, but we are also seeking and receiving life that was in Jesus. He lived it for us. It was poured out in

His death so that it would live on in us. I have written about my own first experience of seeing the life-giving effect of a blood transfusion on a dying young woman.* That was years ago, when I was still a student. I can still see the transparent whiteness of her skin and her pale lips, the absence of a pulse and of breathing. She looked like an alabaster saint. I was sure she had been brought in too late. To me, she was dead. Then a bottle of blood was suspended on a stand beside the bed and a large needle put into her vein, through which the blood— someone else's blood—began to flow.

My own heart was pounding with the drama of what I was seeing. A second and a third bottle followed the first, and somewhere along the way a flush began to appear in her cheeks, and I was able to detect a thready pulse at her wrist. She took a deep sighing breath, and then another. She opened her eyes and looked straight at me. "I'm thirsty," she said. I ran to get some water and spilled a little in my clumsy hurry to meet the first request of a person who had come alive from the dead.

My first thought at that time was to wonder if I could find the donor of that first bottle of blood. Somebody should tell him that part of his own life had raised a young woman from death and was now living in her. Most donated blood, these days, is used early during operations to sustain life where loss of blood is expected. Or it may be to correct severe anemia. These are important uses, but every now and then it becomes part of the battle between life and death, and it is then that we can actually see that blood is life indeed.

I have often wished that blood transfusions had been practiced in New Testament days. How easily the people would have understood it if Jesus had said, "Come to me, you who are dying, and let me give you life. My blood will flow into your veins, and you will live."

---

* See Dr. Brand's book, *In His Image*, for more details about this incident.

Jesus was teaching a profound spiritual truth, and He illustrated it with the best physical illustration that was available to Him at that time. His concern was that the people should understand the reality of shared life, or transferred life, as well as that of sacrifice. In all His parables and metaphors, Jesus used things that were familiar to His hearers. In doing so, He sometimes referred to things that are obscure to us today. His words have a layer of meaning that would have been more accessible to His listeners than to us.

When a person eats blood, the acid in the stomach and the digestive juices in the intestines break down the cells into their basic proteins and then into amino acids and sugars. By the time they are actually absorbed into the bloodstream of the person who is eating, they are just like most of the other building blocks or fuel that the body uses. There is extra iron, but otherwise blood is received into the living body in a form that is not recognized as blood. It is just food, like beans or eggs.

However, the Israelites didn't know about organic chemistry, and they, along with everybody else, thought of ingested blood as being absorbed into their systems as blood itself, so that it would function as blood in the person who ate it. So Jesus used the symbol of eating and drinking to teach them the spiritual truth that His life wouldn't only be laid down for them in sacrifice but would be shared with them in a new quality of their lives.

In a transfusion, that is exactly what blood does. The quality of the blood of the donor is passed on to make up for what is missing in the one who receives it. If a person is anemic, it is no use giving him a transfusion from another anemic person. We look for somebody with blood that is rich in hemoglobin. In a spiritual sense, it was important that Jesus had spiritual health so that He could help those who do not have it.

When we first started work in India, we did not have a blood bank, so we had to use the old-fashioned way of transfusion, which is really the most dramatic and meaningful to watch. This is arm-to-arm transfusion. We used it for emergencies, as when a woman had a serious hemorrhage at childbirth. After we had checked the bloods for compatibility, the donor would lie on a high table and the dying person on a lower table. We used a tube that had a needle on each end. The doctor would put a needle into a vein of the healthy person and the other needle into the vein of the one who was in need. Life would flow from one into the other.

Arm-to-arm transfusion was a personal thing. The donor was usually a relative and was able to watch the life and strength coming back into the face and limbs of the loved one.

In those days the most common reason for giving blood was to revive life. If the total volume of blood is too low, the heart becomes ineffective because it has nothing to pump on. The body is able to restore volume fairly quickly by borrowing fluids from the tissues, but it takes much longer to rebuild the cells. It is the red cells that the body misses soonest. They are the ones that have the wonderful protein called hemoglobin, which is able to carry oxygen from the lungs to all the tissues of the body. On the return trip the same red cells carry the spent oxygen (carbon dioxide) back to the lungs to be breathed out. The brain cannot live without oxygen for more than a few minutes, so if there are not enough red cells, it is an emergency.

Blood, however, is more than survival. It is nourishment and cleansing, and it is also defense.

SHARING NOURISHMENT

This book is about nourishment, and we have discussed the source of our spiritual food as well as its preparation and digestion and absorption. There is another aspect to food that we have not mentioned so far, and that is its distribution.

In the economy of the human body, some cells are well-placed to get a lot of food, but some are busy doing things that don't produce food. They have to depend on others to do the getting. It is the bloodstream that brings nourishment to every living cell, making sure that none are left out.

The lining cells of the intestines wait at the receiving portals for all the fresh food. There the villi reach out into the latest meal that is being digested. They could pick out all the tidbits for themselves, but they know, as all the cells know, that their job is to serve others. They do it by means of the blood. Like a great conveyor belt, the blood receives food from the digestion department and carries it to the eyes, the heart, and the muscles, each of which has only to reach across and take whatever it needs for energy, for activity, or for growth.

In the body of Christ, we all work together to energize each other, but it is the blood of Christ that is the symbol of our dependence on each other and on the Savior who gave us life in the first place.

Behind all the symbols is the reality. Jesus came to give His life for us, and we need to thank Him for both aspects of that gift. His blood was shed. That was the sacrifice of the atonement. But His blood was also shared. It remains a continuing life to be lived in us. The communion service should be a reminder of both aspects. By drinking the wine we symbolize taking it in to be a continuing cleansing and energizing and overcoming influence in our day-to-day lives.

THE BODY'S JANITORIAL SERVICE

While guests at a feast are enjoying themselves, it's easy to forget that somebody has to clean up. Living cells, members of the body, not only receive their nourishment from the blood, they depend on the same blood to clean up after them.

We often fail to appreciate the help we get from others until one day they are missing and we have to take care of things ourselves. That is how we learn about the important functions of the body. We find out the function of an organ by noting what trouble there is when it fails. When body cells have been working and using up food, there are two common residues left over. One is carbon dioxide, and the other is urea. These are end products of the breakdown of sugars and proteins. There is no way they can be used any further, so they have to be thrown out, or they clog up the whole system. This is where the blood comes in. Having delivered its good things, it carries away the garbage.

The carbon dioxide is carried off to the lungs, where it is breathed out. The urea is taken to the kidneys, which filter the blood and send the urea and other residues to the bladder and out, as urine.

Muscles use a lot of energy as they work for us. They also produce a lot of residue. The harder they work, the faster the residue must be carried away, or the muscles go into painful spasms and cramps. Old people sometimes get a narrowing of their arteries, especially in their legs. This cuts down the amount of blood that can flow in to supply the muscles and also the amount of residue they can carry away. If you see an elderly man walking a few steps and then resting a minute before walking on a few more steps and resting again, you can be pretty sure he has narrowed blood vessels and has to wait for the garbage to be taken out before he can go on walking. He stops because he feels the cramp beginning in his calf, so he waits for the blood to come by with its oxygen and its trash pick-up.

I used to think it strange that the Bible keeps talking about the cleansing power of the blood (1 Peter 1:2). It seemed to me that blood was messy stuff. I needed to wash my white coats if they became stained with blood. Today I love the analogy; it is so literally true of the body. The blood is constantly cleansing every cell and washing away all the debris that accumulates all the time. I like Paul's phrase in Hebrews 9:14 (KJV), "How much more shall the blood of Christ ... purge your conscience from dead works?" This is exactly what my blood does in my body. It cleanses all my tissues from the residues of past work. When I, as a Christian, try to do good work, I find it hard to be pure either in motive or in action. I offer my work to the Lord, saying, "Lord, I tried to do your will. Cleanse me from all the residues that have accumulated from even the best that I can do. As your blood flows through me, cleanse me from my dead works to serve the living God."

POWER IN THE BLOOD

So blood is life, it is energy, and it is cleansing. The Bible uses another word about the function of blood. In Revelation, John says he saw a war in heaven. It was a battle between that old serpent, the devil, the deceiver, fighting against Michael and the angels. Finally, the battle was over, and Satan was cast out. It says that he was overcome "by the blood of the Lamb" (Revelation 12:11).

The forces of evil defeated by the blood of Jesus? Does blood fight? How can it overcome?

In chapter 7, which is about mother's milk, I commented that a mother is able to convey to her baby, in her milk, some of the antibodies that she has developed in her blood when she has needed to fight germs that have attacked her. Now we need to take a look at the battles that go on in the blood of every healthy person.

When I was a student, we knew little about the immune system. We knew that there were cells in the blood that helped to defend us against disease, but exactly what they did and how they did it was a mystery. Today, immunology is a whole science to itself, and knowledge of the details of the defenses of the body is growing all the time.

Along with red cells that carry oxygen and big white cells that move into infected areas to fight any foreign germ they can find, the bloodstream carries billions of little round white cells that are called lymphocytes. As students, we knew that these cells multiplied when people suffered from infections, but we did not know why or what they did. Today we know much more. They have been given a variety of names, such as T lymphocytes for the ones that grow in the thymus gland and B lymphocytes, which are made in the bone marrow, and lots of others.

I must share just one facet of the skills of the T lymphocytes, because I get excited at the ingenuity that must have gone into their design and because I'm so happy to have these little guys on my side when I am sick.

Bacteria and viruses have strange shapes. Their surfaces have bumps and hollows and points of vulnerability and areas of strength. Every type of germ has a different shape and a different sort of shell. My T lymphocytes spend their lives traveling around the body in the bloodstream, wherever it takes them. They also concentrate in places where most germs try to get into the body. The tonsils are made up of masses of lymphocytes standing guard at the entrance gates of the lungs, where streams of air often carry germs into places where it is fairly easy to squeeze through into the body. It is never long before an invading germ meets a T lymphocyte. The first wonderful thing is that the lymphocyte knows at once that this living cell is not "one of us." It is an enemy. How it knows, nobody knows. Is it smell? It is too dark to see and too quiet to hear. But it knows.

The next wonderful thing is what it does. It inspects the enemy cell and takes a template, or pattern, of its surface, noting especially the weak points. Then our friend runs back to the factory where new cells are made and announces the emergency. "An enemy has entered the body and is rapidly multiplying. I know just where its weak spots are. We have to manufacture antibodies of exactly this shape so that the enemy will be killed and no other cells will be harmed."

An older lymphocyte may hurry up at this point and tell the factory that the shape of the needed antibodies is exactly the same as was used a year ago, when there was a brief war in the body during the flu season. Therefore there is no need to repeat the time-consuming preparation of the prototype anti-bodies. We already have them. All that is needed is to rush into mass production. Thus, before the virus has time to do any real harm, masses of specific antibodies are all over the body, overcoming every last virus and restoring health and whole-ness everywhere.

When the battle has been won, it does not mean the war is over. It is always possible that the same kind of virus may attack again, months or years later. It would be wasteful and would burden the blood if all the billions of new antibodies were to remain in the blood, just in case exactly the same kind of virus came again. Each new infection would fill up the bloodstream with a new load of antibodies, until there was no room for anything except defense. On the other hand, it is a pity to waste the knowledge of the exact pattern of the virus and of the antibodies that would be needed if it came again.

So, in some mysterious way, just a few of the lymphocytes that took the imprint of the virus have a sort of immortality conferred upon them. While all other cells in the blood have a short life span and are replaced, the cells that carry the special defense information live on to a ripe old age, ready to recognize their own specific enemy and then to inform all the young cells who have never done this before just how to make the antibodies they need to win the new battle.

Physicians have long known that people who have had infections before are able to recover more quickly the next time they are attacked. They also know that such people can meet the infection and overcome it even without getting sick at all. They knew this about smallpox long before vaccination was practiced. They said that one attack of smallpox (or measles or typhoid) protected against a second attack. They had a nice phrase to describe people who had been exposed to many infections and were able to overcome almost any epidemic: "He has wise blood."

Those old physicians didn't know anything about cells or the thymus gland or the bone marrow with its factories for immune cells and antibodies. They just observed the effects of a system that even today we find too complex to fathom. Now, with a better understanding of immunology, we use "wise blood" to inject into people who are about to enter danger areas where they may become exposed to germs they have never met. We give them blood serum extracts to impart wisdom to their blood, wisdom and experience that have been acquired by somebody else who has been there before and has overcome those same infections ahead of time.

This is the picture behind the second chapter of Hebrews. That chapter ends with this statement about Jesus: "Because he himself suffered when he was tempted, he is able to help those who are being tempted" (Hebrews 2:18). This help is not just an instruction manual. It is an alliance. It is the rich blood of Jesus Christ. It is His life living in me and helping me to meet temptation and overcome it.

When we take the cup at the communion feast and drink the wine, we remember two things: Jesus, whose blood was shed in the sacrifice for my sin; and Jesus, who lived to enrich His blood by facing temptation for me and now shares with me His power to energize, to cleanse, and to help me to overcome in my life the same kind of temptations He overcame in His life.

There is *power* in the blood.

CHAPTER 18

The Lord's Breakfast

"Simon son of John, do you truly love me more than these?"

JOHN 21:15

The story of this meal is well known. Jesus served bread and fish on the beach after the disciples had been fishing all night. No big deal. In the life of Peter, however, and perhaps of all the others, it may have been the decisive meal of their whole lives. In their memory it may have had as much significance as the Lord's Supper a few days before. To me also it has a special poignancy and needs to be celebrated again and again.

To understand it we need to go back through all the rollercoaster sequence of emotions the disciples had experienced. Let's follow Peter as typical of the group of fishermen. After all, it was his idea to go on the fishing trip that started the adventure that ended in the Lord's Breakfast.

It all began when Jesus came into their lives. Peter was a professional fisherman. Rough and tough, he worked hard, and he shared in the hopes and fears of all his neighbors who lived under the yoke of the Roman rulers of Israel. He shared their resentment of servitude, and he shared their faith that one day God would say that His people had been punished enough and would send the Messiah to lead them into deliverance. The Romans would be conquered and expelled from the land, and the Messiah would introduce a new era of righteousness and prosperity.

Everyone knew the transition wouldn't be easy. There would be fighting and bloodshed. Many Israelites would die, but it would all be worth it. When Jesus appeared and began to speak and preach with authority and the people saw that He had the power to do miracles, it was natural that people would think that the Messiah had come.

It took real courage for Peter to give up his boats, his nets, and fishing and follow Jesus. As one of the first disciples of Jesus, no doubt he thought he would be in the vanguard of the fighting. He might be killed, but the risk was worth it, for if he survived he would be a leader in the new kingdom.

He was puzzled at the lack of military preparations but recognized that people had to repent and turn humbly to God in order to be accepted as His own people and be granted victory and freedom. During those three years of close fellowship with Jesus, Peter had moments of insight into the nature of the one he came to recognize as the Son of God. He went along with the humble servant role that Jesus adopted, thinking no doubt that this was a pose to avoid suspicion of his intentions of conquest. He reacted strongly against Jesus when He spoke of coming suffering and death, which Peter felt was going too far.

Then came the reality of judgment and crucifixion. This must have been absolutely shattering. All that Peter had believed and lived for was falling around him. Terrified now of being identified as a member of a rebel band, he tried to distance himself from any connection with Jesus, the condemned. When Jesus looked at him on His way out of the judgment hall, Peter went out and wept bitterly. He wept tears of bereavement for a loved one and tears of frustration for three years lost out of his life. Yet there was still a glimmer of hope. God might send angels and save Jesus from the cross.

Even up to the end, even when Jesus had spoken at the Last Supper of His coming death, the hope was that if this crisis were somehow to pass, Jesus would prove to be the Messiah after all. Then the disciples would be in positions of power and authority in His kingdom. For this reason, at the Last Supper they were still arguing about which of them would be the greatest.

The lowest point came when Jesus actually died. Everybody saw it happen. He handed over His responsibilities as eldest son to the disciple John, and then He cried out, "It is finished" and died. With that death, all hope died in Peter's heart.

On the first day of the week, the unbelievable happened. Rumors flew from mouth to mouth. He is risen! The women have seen him! Peter races with John down to the tomb and finds it empty. They all gather in a locked room with wild uncertainty and hope. Then, there He is. Scarred and marked and wounded—but alive! From absolute despair, their own earlier hopes struggled to come to life again. This was the Messiah. The kingdom could be a reality. Never again the shame, the degradation, the poverty, and the rejection they had willingly endured because of the hope to come.

Then Jesus spoke. We cannot realize the disappointment of those words unless we put ourselves into the mindset of Peter and the others who had experienced the mood swings of the past few hours. Jesus held out His hands, still bearing the ugly wounds of His crucifixion and said, "As the Father has sent me, I am sending you" (John 20:21).

THE MOMENT OF TRUTH

Only with the background of hopes and dreams can we understand the impact on Peter of those first words from Jesus.

Jesus made it clear that there was to be no glorious future for this band of disciples. He was leaving. There was to be no victory over the Romans, no thrones or crowns. They wouldn't even have the supporting presence of Jesus. Peter and the others were to continue to live and work as Jesus had lived; they would continue to experience rejection, poverty, persecution, possibly death. Peter's mind, already in an emotional whirl, simply couldn't cope with this new mixture of delight at the resurrection and dismay at the prospect of a continuing life of persecution without his leader and with no prospect of victory at the end.

I feel sure that at that moment a new idea was forming in Peter's mind. I think it would have formed in mine, if I had been in his position. He may have thought, "I never bargained for this. I agreed to follow Jesus, and I will follow Him, so long as He is here to follow. As for the future, when He has gone, that is a new situation for which I have made no commitment. I wonder if my old skill as a fisherman is still with me. I can always go back to my boat and my nets. At least *I must have time to think.* Too much has happened at once. A night on the lake will be a help." Aloud, he said, "I am going fishing tonight." The others, perhaps feeling the same need to adjust to all that had been happening, responded, "We'll come along too."

A moment of truth comes to all of us at some time. I remember my wedding. I had the loveliest girl to marry. I had thought about it for a long time. I knew some other nice girls, and it had taken me quite a while to ask the one I did. Now the date was set, and all the family and friends had been invited. I had rented my suit and hat and was all dressed up. My best man was saying it was time to go up front and wait for the bride and her father.

Then suddenly it hit me. *This was it!* There was no going back! This was for life. I had nowhere to run. There was no looking back. I felt a sort of panic, which lasted all the way up the aisle. A few minutes later, there she was! Radiant in white. She slipped her hand into mine, and I had a new moment of truth, not of doubt this time but of sheer delight. I had her; she was mine. There was no going back for her, and we belonged to each other forever and ever. I was at peace.

Jesus had His moment of truth when John the Baptist said, "Look, the Lamb of God, who takes away the sin of the world!" The temptation in the wilderness was all about His acceptance of His moment of truth.

The words, "As the father has sent me, *I am sending you*," framed Peter's moment of truth. The night of fishing was his time of temptation in the wilderness, his chance to run away. Perhaps he thought that he would feel all his old skill and pride in fishing coming back to him. He would feel the tug on the net and see several fish being pulled into the boat; he would know that he could still do it. He could still make money. He was still master of his craft and of his life. He could start again.

That night they caught nothing.

In the early dawn the disciples looked to the shore and saw a fire of coals and a man standing beside it. He called out to them, "Had any luck? Have you caught anything?"

"Nothing!"

"Cast your net on the other side of the ship!" A sudden shoal of fish. Panic, as a swarm of great fish threatened to break the net and get loose. "Help! Lend a hand, you guys; we've got a record catch."

It is the *Lord*! Peter threw himself into the sea, swam, and waded ashore. The boat followed, dragging the net with 153 *great fish*, which were then piled on the beach. What a catch! But the master fisherman was the Lord, not Peter or the other professionals. Jesus had some fish already on the grill, and some bread. "Bring some of the fish you've just caught," said Jesus, "and come. Let's have some breakfast!" There in the dawn, they clustered around the fire. Peter had the feeling that a whole new reality was closing in on him. This was a new moment.

THE DAWNING OF A NEW DAY

"Simon, son of John, do you truly love me more than these?"

I have never known just what that question meant. It seems to me that there are three possible meanings.

It could have meant, "Peter, do you really love me more than these others love me?" This might have been a reference to the time before the crucifixion when Peter had said, "Even if all fall away, I will not." So was Jesus now gently reminding Peter that, in spite of his proud boast, he had indeed denied Him? So did Peter still want to say that he loved Jesus more than these others loved Him?

It might have meant, "Do you love me more than you love these other friends?" Peter had chosen to go out fishing with his old friends rather than to stay with Jesus and find out just what He had meant by saying, "I am sending you." Perhaps he would rather have them than Jesus.

Then I think of the beach, and I realize that the whole area must have been dominated by the sight and smell of that great pile of fish. To Peter, 153 big fish must have meant a lot of money. It would be a day of excellent business; it might foreshadow a prosperous career in fishing. Jesus might have been looking at all those fish and the dollar signs above them. He might have waved His hand toward them and asked, "Peter, do you love me more than *these*? Are you willing to give up your profession to follow me and live in poverty and even as a fugitive, when you could be a respected fisherman?"

The most striking thing about that breakfast is that Peter had changed. The turbulent experiences of the past few days had taught him two important things. He had learned his own weakness. There was no boastful statement about his love or his courage or about being better than anybody else. He didn't even presume to use the same word for love in his answer as Jesus had used in His question. Jesus asked, "Do you love [*agapao*] me?" meaning devoted self-giving love. Peter answered, "I love [*phileo*] you" meaning, "Yes, I love you as your friend."

The second thing Peter had learned, perhaps while he had been fishing, was that he really did love Jesus and that he needed Him, and that even a life as a servant was acceptable if Jesus was to be the master. I don't think Peter ever forgot that breakfast picnic on the beach. It was the time that questions were finally answered and commitments were made.

A SPIRITUAL OXYMORON

Richard Foster tells of an occasion at the Keswick convention in England long ago. It is vivid to me because I was there when that great Scottish Bible teacher, Graham Scroggie, was leading some of the services in that wonderful annual Christian convention. He was a born teacher and a master of the English language, with his rolling Scottish accent. Yet, as all truly eloquent people do, he used simple words.

Scroggie was leading the missionary meeting in the smaller of the two great tents in Keswick, wearing, as he always did, the academic gown of his university. He gave the missionary challenge, followed by prayer. Some in the audience stood to offer themselves for service, and then the meeting concluded. Graham Scroggie stayed at the front until all had left, except for one young woman who just continued sitting, thoughtfully and by herself. Graham went up to her and asked if there was anything he could do to help her or clarify something he had said. "No," she replied, "I think I know what God wants me to do, but I cannot seem to make up my mind whether to do it."

"Oh," said Scroggie, "I think you need to come with me to Joppa and see what Peter said." He turned the leaves of his Bible to the tenth chapter of Acts and pointed to the story of Peter on the rooftop, when he saw the sheet let down, full of animals, and the voice of God told him to rise, kill, and eat. His reply had been, "No, Lord, I have never eaten anything common or unclean."

Scroggie said, "You know, there is something strange about Peter's reply to God. He said, 'No, Lord.' Now that is not really a proper sentence at all. Peter could have said no, and that would have been a statement. Or he could have just said 'Lord!' and that would have meant yes! But you just cannot say 'No' and then finish by saying 'Lord.' Those words do not belong together."

Scroggie then wrote on a piece of paper in capital letters the words NO, LORD, put it on his Bible, and gave it to the lady on her lap. He said, "I think that is what you are trying to say. Now I am going to leave you and go over there to pray for you. I want you to pray too and then take this pencil and cross out one of those words."

He hardly had time to kneel down when the Lord told him it was time to go back. He went to her and saw that the word NO had been crossed out. She was sitting back in her chair, crying and repeating to herself, "Jesus is Lord, Jesus is Lord, Jesus is Lord." That was her moment of truth. For her, that was the Lord's Breakfast. That was when she knew decisions had to be made and she made them—decisions from which there was no turning back.

RENEWING OUR VOWS

I love to celebrate the Lord's Supper. I take the bread and the wine. I am reminded of the body of Christ, of His sacrifice for me, and of His continuing life in me—cleansing, overcoming. I also need to celebrate the Lord's Breakfast. I need to remind myself of my commitment. Just as my wife and I celebrate our marriage vows each year and thank God for all that we mean to each other, so I need to remind myself of my commitment to my Lord. I need to ask myself, and ask Him, too, whether I have grown slack or forgetful. I need to hear Him say to me, "Do you love me more than *these*?" And I need to search out and see if any of those things have crept into my life and claimed my loyalty. I have to find out what they might be and put them down into second place or abolish them because they have come to constitute a continuing challenge to my first loyalty. Then I can truly say, "Yes, Lord, you know I love you."

Then I can go ahead and eat my bread and broiled fish. I can discuss the details of the day or of my direction in life because now there is no tension. Once loyalties are settled, all other priorities fall into place. There is peace. That kind of unhurried breakfast is the best meal of the day.

I began this book with the story of my best meal. That meal and this meal have features in common. Both started with the failure of fishermen to catch fish. Both had broiled fish and bread to eat in the end. My best meal in India, eaten beside the water, began, as is our custom, with prayer for God's blessing on our food and for His presence with us as we ate.

The Lord's Breakfast on the beach began with His presence and with the recognition of His lordship. It continued with love and fellowship that had finally been restored after severe testing. The night of temptation was over; the food was simple and fresh. Peter began his meal, still uncertain about his future. He ended it, a trusted officer with a commission.

There is something special about breakfasts. It is a shame that so many of them are rushed, as people wake up late and just grab some coffee on their way to work or school. Even if we find—*especially* if we find—that an unhurried breakfast is not practical every day, I do urge that at regular intervals each of us make a point to have a Lord's Breakfast. The features that make a breakfast deserve that title are, first, that it should be unhurried. Those who share the meal should be likeminded with us, in our love of the Lord. The conversation, or meditation if we are alone, should concern practical matters related to commitment.

I believe churches should do this from time to time. We all have potluck suppers. Breakfasts have a different atmosphere. People are more ready to do business over breakfast, more ready to make decisions. Jesus chose the early hours of the day for some of the prayers that meant the most in His life. He is ready to meet us as we seek His presence and renew our vows at the *Lord's* Breakfast.

NOTE TO THE READER

The publisher invites you to share your response to the message of this book by writing Discovery House Publishers, P.O. Box 3566, Grand Rapids, MI 49501, USA or by calling 1-800-653-8333. For information about other Discovery House books, music, or DVDs, contact us at the same address or phone number. Find us on the Internet at http://www.dhp.org/ or send an e-mail to books@dhp.org.